ASPATORE
C-Level Business Intelligence™

Praise for Books, Business Intelligence Publications & Services

"What C-Level executives read to keep their edge and make pivotal business decisions. Timeless classics for indispensable knowledge." - Richard Costello, Manager-Corporate Marketing Communication, General Electric (NYSE: GE)

"True insight from the doers in the industry, as opposed to the critics on the sideline." - Steve Hanson, CEO, On Semiconductor (NASDAQ: ONNN)

"Unlike any other business books, Inside the Minds captures the essence, the deep-down thinking processes, of people who make things happen." - Martin Cooper, CEO, Arraycomm

"The only useful way to get so many good minds speaking on a complex topic." - Scott Bradner, Senior Technical Consultant, Harvard University

"Tremendous insights...a must read..." - James Quinn, Litigation Chair, Weil, Gotshal & Manges

"Great information for business executives and employers of any size." - Judy Langevin, Employment Chair, Gray, Plant, Mooty, Mooty & Bennett

"A rare peek behind the curtains and into the minds of the industry's best." - Brandon Baum, Partner, Cooley Godward

"Intensely personal, practical advice from seasoned dealmakers." - Mary Ann Jorgenson, Coordinator of Business Practice Area, Squire, Sanders & Dempsey

INSIDE THE MINDS

**Empowering Professionals of All Levels
With C-Level Business Intelligence**
www.InsideTheMinds.com

The critically acclaimed *Inside the Minds* series provides readers of all levels with proven business intelligence from C-Level executives (CEO, CFO, CTO, CMO, Partner) from the world's most respected companies. Each chapter is comparable to a white paper or essay and is a future-oriented look at where an industry/profession/topic is heading and the most important issues for future success. Each author has been carefully chosen through an exhaustive selection process by the *Inside the Minds* editorial board to write a chapter for this book. *Inside the Minds* was conceived in order to give readers actual insights into the leading minds of business executives worldwide. Because so few books or other publications are actually written by executives in industry, *Inside the Minds* presents an unprecedented look at various industries and professions never before available.

For information on bulk orders, sponsorship opportunities or any other questions, please email store@aspatore.com.

For information on licensing the content in this book, or any content published by Aspatore, please email jonp@aspatore.com.

To nominate yourself, another individual, or a group of executives for an upcoming Inside the Minds book, or to suggest a specific topic for an Inside the Minds book, please email jason@aspatore.com.

ASPATORE
C-Level Business Intelligence™

Publisher of Books, Business Intelligence Publications & Services
www.Aspatore.com

Aspatore is the world's largest and most exclusive publisher of C-Level executives (CEO, CFO, CTO, CMO, Partner) from the world's most respected companies. Aspatore annually publishes C-Level executives from over half the Global 500, top 250 law firms (MPs/Chairs), and other leading companies of all sizes in books, essays, briefings, white papers and other publications. By focusing on publishing only C-Level executives, Aspatore provides professionals of all levels with proven business intelligence from industry insiders, rather than relying on the knowledge of unknown authors and analysts. Aspatore publishes an innovative line of business intelligence resources including Inside the Minds, Bigwig Briefs, ExecRecs, Business Travel Bible, Brainstormers, The C-Level Test, and Aspatore Business Reviews, in addition to other best selling business books, briefs and essays. Aspatore also provides an array of business services including the Aspatore Electronic Library, PIA Reports, ExecEnablers, and The C-Level Review, as well as outsourced business library and researching capabilities. Aspatore focuses on traditional print publishing and providing business intelligence services, while our portfolio companies, Corporate Publishing Group (B2B writing & editing) and Aspatore Business Intelligence (business intelligence stores) focus on developing areas within the business and publishing worlds.

CORPORATE PUBLISHING GROUP

Outsource Your Company's Writing & Editing To the World's Best
www.CorporatePublishingGroup.com

Corporate Publishing Group (CPG) provides companies with on-demand writing and editing resources from the world's best writing teams. Our clients come to CPG for the writing and editing of books, reports, speeches, company brochures, press releases, product literature, web site copy and other publications. This enables companies to save time and money, reduce headcount, and ensure polished and articulate written pieces. Each client is assigned a CPG team devoted to their company, which works on their projects throughout the course of a year on an as-needed basis and helps generate new written documents, review and edit documents already written, and provide an outside perspective before a document "goes public" in order to help companies maintain a polished image both internally and externally. Clients have included companies in all industries and disciplines, ranging from financial to technology to law firms, and are represented by over half of the Fortune 500. For more information please e-mail rpollock@corporateapublishinggroup.com or visit our web site at www.CorporatePublishingGroup.com.

INSIDE THE MINDS

INSIDE THE MINDS:
The Automotive Industry
The Future of the Automotive Industry: Opportunities, Risks & Areas to Watch

ASPATORE
C-Level Business Intelligence™

> If you are interested in forming a business partnership with Aspatore or licensing the content in this book (for publications, web sites, educational materials), purchasing bulk copies for your team/company with your company logo, or for sponsorship, promotions or advertising opportunities, please email store@aspatore.com or call toll free 1-866-Aspatore.

Published by Aspatore, Inc.
For corrections, company/title updates, comments or any other inquiries please email info@aspatore.com.

First Printing, November 2002
10 9 8 7 6 5 4 3 2 1

Copyright © 2002 by Aspatore Books, Inc. All rights reserved. Printed in the United States of America. No part of this publication may be reproduced or distributed in any form or by any means, or stored in a database or retrieval system, except as permitted under Sections 107 or 108 of the United States Copyright Act, without prior written permission of the publisher.

ISBN 1-58762-065-0

Inside the Minds Managing Editor, Carolyn Murphy, Edited by Jo Alice Hughes, Proofread by Ginger Conlon, Cover design by Kara Yates & Ian Mazie

Material in this book is for educational purposes only. This book is sold with the understanding that neither any of the authors or the publisher is engaged in rendering medical, legal, accounting, investment, or any other professional service. For legal advice, please consult your personal lawyer.

This book is printed on acid free paper.

A special thanks to all the individuals that made this book possible.

Special thanks to: Kirsten Catanzano, Melissa Conradi, Molly Logan, Justin Hallberg

The views expressed by the individuals in this book (or the individuals on the cover) do not necessarily reflect the views shared by the companies they are employed by (or the companies mentioned in this book). The companies referenced may not be the same company that the individual works for since the publishing of this book.

HD9710.A2 I57 2002

0134106511485

Inside the minds : the automotive industry : c2002.

2004 03 22

INSIDE THE MINDS:
The Auto Industry
The Future of the Automotive Industry: Opportunities, Risks & Areas to Watch

CONTENTS

Irma B. Elder   9
A PASSION FOR BUSINESS AND PEOPLE

Don Walker   27
FLEXIBILITY IN THE FACE OF CHANGE

Vic Edelbrock   53
THE IMPORTANCE OF KNOWING THE BUSINESS

Linda Hasenfratz   67
MANAGING OPPORTUNITIES IN THE AUTO INDUSTRY

Scott L. Thompson   83
LESSONS IN AUTOMOTIVE ENTREPRENEURSHIP

Nancy L. Gioia   99
*EXCITING AND CHALLENGING
ELEMENTS OF THE AUTOMOTIVE
INDUSTRY*

Richard Colliver   123
*MEETING THE DEMANDS OF
TOMORROW'S CONSUMERS*

J. D. Power, III   135
*THE BIG PICTURE: UNDERSTANDING
CUSTOMER EXPECTATIONS*

Acknowledgements and Dedications   159

A PASSION FOR BUSINESS AND PEOPLE

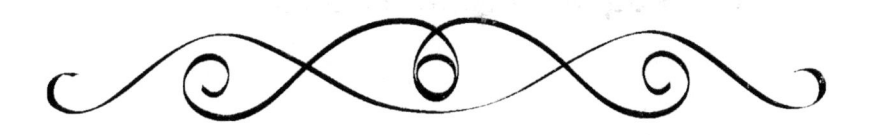

Irma B. Elder

Elder Automotive Group

Chief Executive Officer

Being, Doing, and Hiring the Best

I have a passion for the automotive industry. I think everything about it is exciting. I am exhilarated when our sales are good and strong. Every aspect of the business is intriguing to me, every moment, both the tough times and especially the good times.

I am going to repeat myself. I have a passion for the business. I have been very lucky because I feel I have an affinity for numbers, a vital trait for success in our industry -- any industry, for that matter. I learned by studying spreadsheets until they became second nature to me. My first days in the business were long and trying, but I still found the time to bring those spreadsheets home, spread them around the family room, and thoroughly study every entry until I really understood what it all meant.

I also love the personal contact, the quality part of the business that is so important to success. I consider myself very fortunate, but fortune doesn't come easily. We are all given choices in life; sometimes our choices work for us, and sometimes they don't. If they don't work, then we have to make other choices or live with what we have chosen. I advise everybody to never give up. I have fallen so many times, and often I didn't think I could get up again. But I did, and I know I will be challenged over and over again. Everyone who owns a business today is challenged. When this happens, I dig down deep inside myself to find the courage to face whatever comes my way.

I don't pretend to be someone different from who I truly am. When I talk about our cars, I tell people I love the products we sell because I really do. I welcome their arrival from the factory and savor the feeling of contentment when they depart the dealerships with their new owners, our customers.

I live every day with excitement and enthusiasm because I can't find anything else I enjoy doing as much. I come alive when I'm at the offices. I am very shy by nature, although people won't believe that. When I'm in my office or when I'm with business colleagues, I absolutely love every moment. But even then, there's excitement in being so passionate. I enjoy my business and industry to the fullest. When I walk in and smile at somebody and say, "Good morning," they will respond.

I am often asked about my employees and how they are motivated. I work hard at motivation, first with the managers, who in turn work with their own staffs. I study the financial statements. I ask questions, and I probe inconsistencies. I do a great deal of public relations, networking, and community relations. I don't ask anyone to do anything I would not do myself. I am not a tough manager, but I am much more in control than people realize. I believe in allowing people to do their jobs, but keeping a keen eye on the standards of our organization. Most importantly, I interface with my two sons, officers with the Elder Automotive Group. They are now running many aspects of the various entities our company owns.

I do have a few words of advice. In selecting your staff, you must be able to find the best talent for the appropriate positions, and you must be incredibly honest about their capabilities. Just because you know someone personally, you cannot fool yourself into pretending that the person will do a good job when you know deep inside they are not qualified for that particular situation. Allow people to do their jobs, but keep them accountable. Look for passion, confidence, and the team player who believes in the same things you do.

Respect your employees for their initiative and for what they do best, for working independently and as part of a team. Respect is an important word in management. Give it, and you will receive it many times over in return. By focusing on their strengths, interests, and talents, we use people in their best capacities. Play "matchmaker" with people and appropriate employment positions, and you will be gratified when the match is perfect.

Our managers are people who care and who are passionate about their staff and their customers. They are also held accountable for their departments. This is how our teams are developed, and they function accordingly. This way, we have the same vision when we plan for the future together.

Goals are very important as well. In building a company's survival plan, you have to have achievable goals. I have forced myself to learn how to plan. I'm the type of person who likes to think on her feet. However, I have taught myself that to build the company and to survive in one of the most complex industries, goals and planning are essential. I meet with my sons and we set the goals. While we share the identical vision, our means to reach the goals may be different. We all understand that. I first strive to gain an understanding of their ideas and communicate mine. I need to listen to them. They need to listen to me. We then sell the plan to our management team, whom we ask for feedback and strategies for implementation.

Leading by Example

To become a leader, you have to start from the bottom and learn every detail of the business you are running. You have to have an affinity for the people with whom you work. You have to be knowledgeable about what you do, and you have to do it well. Above all, you have to have integrity and honesty.

The Automotive Industry

I lead by example. I visit all corners of the business, empower my managers, conduct and attend meetings in the dealerships and at the manufacturers' corporate headquarters. I talk to my customers, bring them coffee, infuse the hospitality concept for which we are known. I savor the personal interface with people. I have a habit in the late afternoon or evening of going to the showroom, meeting the customers, and talking with them. I want to make everyone feel welcome. I want them to know I am a good listener. I try to make every one of them feel important because they are important.

The financial stability of the company, the quality of the people, and the quality of service we give our customers are three things I have to keep my fingers on. I can plug into my computer every day and see what every one of my businesses has done up to the day before. I'm right on top of it, so I know the financial stability we have, and I know what our weaknesses are. I don't want to know at the end of the month, or at the end of the week, or at the end of two days. I want to know right now. This way, I can see where we might possibly have a weakness, and I can talk to our people and advisors about it.

I consider success surviving every day in the automotive business. Success means a healthy bottom line due to productive, contented employees and satisfied customers.

Challenges of Leadership in the Auto Industry

The cycle of change in this business and the economy challenge us every day. The automotive industry is a major balancing act. The costs of goods and services are rising. It is becoming increasingly difficult to maintain strong profit margins. Customers are concerned with price and product. We rely on the manufacturers to provide us with new, exciting, innovative, and affordable products to sell. We constantly strive to service the customers' expectations. Economics and lifestyles change very rapidly. These are normal changes, some anticipated, some unexpected. All are challenging, nevertheless.

The Automotive Industry

I maintain we always have a turbulent economy. I manage the same way, turbulent or not. I always try to stay positive, so I can transfer the positive image to our people. Taking a businesslike, optimistic approach sets an example for my employees. I believe you have to be positive in good times. But it is more important to stay positive in bad times. The essential thing is to be consistent, keep encouraging the staff, and keep a constant cash flow. We are mindful of how volatile the marketplace is, and we plan accordingly.

Another challenge is determining what risks to take. To grow, we invest and acquire additional properties. Obviously we don't jump into a hornet's nest. We do our homework. I consult with my sons, our managers, our CPA, and our attorneys. They assess the risks and communicate their findings. I believe this is the way it should be done. However, there is an intuition based on experience that goes with the territory. Over the years, you learn to recognize a good business risk and a solid growth strategy. You depend on your advisors to assist with the fact-finding and decision-making. But ultimately, the buck stops at my desk with my signature. I accept all responsibility for any risks we take. I have the ultimate vote, and I make the final decision to take the risk.

For me, the most challenging part of being a leader is dealing with some of the people you meet along the way. As a leader myself, I get very discouraged when people try to take advantage and are incapable of handling their positions. It bothers me tremendously when I find people who do not keep their promises. We often encounter companies that are less than honest and don't deliver what they promise. When I deal with such people, whom I sometimes have to bring into line, it bothers me.

The one thing I would change about the auto industry is the negative impression some people have of the manufacturers we represent. I think people forget we are persons in this business, human beings with strengths and weaknesses just like everybody else in any other major industry. We are faced daily with issues.

But I wouldn't change the people or the industry's passionate love affair with the automobile. Designers, engineers, executives, dealer principals, salesmen, technicians, and support staff all have this wonderful feeling for their art. The style, color, smell, touch, comfort...everything about the automobile is enthralling.

When I first started in the business, a very special person sent me a plaque that still stands on my desk. It reads, "There is no limit to what a man can do or where he can go if he doesn't mind who gets the credit." That is one of the best pieces of advice that I have been given, and I pass it along to others. In other words, don't allow your ego to destroy you. Let the people get the credit for what they do. Stand back, be happy, and share their success. I believe in allowing other people to get the credit they deserve and in respecting their positions in the business. As a woman, I encourage others not to show your weakness. If you are frightened or angry or upset, try not to show it. If it is getting to the point where you feel as though you are going to be beaten, go somewhere and regroup. Then go back to business and smile. Easy to say, difficult to do, but it can be done.

Customer Service Is Priority One

This is a people business. Taking excellent care of customers is our number one priority. I like to believe that treating people as you would want to be treated should be the primary golden rule. Because we bring people into our showrooms, our service centers and our lives, we need to pay attention to the Elder Automotive Group's mission of integrity, honesty, and hospitality. Customer service is a way of life for us; it is the primary component of everything we do. We serve the people who choose to come to us for some of the most exciting, beautiful automobiles in the world. These customers are the keys to growth and profit.

We take care of our customers by having clean facilities, as well as a knowledgeable and capable sales staff and service technicians. We listen to what our customers tell us. We listen to their concerns, their needs, and their wants. In our Elder Ford store, we have a children's playroom. We have a television set with children's tapes, and we have toys and games. In our service center, we installed a small putting green. It is amazing how many customers like to putt on our indoor green. Even though we have coffee in our service area, we also have a café where people can get coffee and buy refreshments at a nominal cost. All of these services accommodate the customer. Above all, we employ the most knowledgeable service technicians, and we train them to ensure they take care of the products we sell to our customers.

Looking To the Future

The automotive industry is a business I know will survive a hundred years and more. A hundred years is a long time, but look where it began. I know I will not be here, but I hope my family will carry on our traditions of hospitality, integrity, and honesty in all of their endeavors. As the head of a family-owned business, you hand down your life's lessons to your offspring with the hopes and dreams they will hand them to their future generations. Create and lead a strong family unit, fill it with love, and make it fiscally sound. You build a reputation, and they will continue the vision and the mission.

The future is dazzling. New technology emerges daily, as do provisions for environmental responsibility. Technology requires us to provide more training for our technicians. To service the vehicles expediently, it is our responsibility to provide the necessary educational opportunities for our employees to perform their jobs well. New automobiles are being manufactured with so much advanced instrumentation that our technicians have to be properly trained to service the cars we sell.

Our manufacturers have a new initiative to sell premium brands together. For example, Jaguar, Aston Martin, and Land Rover are displayed and sold in the same showroom, in the public eye. This is new to our industry, but is a good, sound strategy and is showing great response with the consumer base nationwide and internationally, as well. We are working to make the experience of purchasing a car effortless, enjoyable, and rewarding for the customer.

To keep up my knowledge of the industry as things are changing, I read and listen to every item I can about the business, lifestyles, and the economy in general. I learn from everyone I meet and from everything I read. I network constantly with both professional and charitable organizations. I meet some of the most incredible, capable, talented, and interesting people wherever I go, and I learn from every one of them. Each thing I do in my life I approach as a learning experience, even sweeping my deck at home, because that teaches me that the most humble of jobs should be done correctly. I try to keep on top of everything that is happening with my industry, from the latest inventions to the environmentally correct procedures we follow in our daily operations.

To position our company for the future, we do an analysis of the marketplace. We adjust by promoting the introduction of new vehicles and by servicing a public with changing attitudes and changing lifestyles. The marketplace should not surprise us; we should anticipate what is happening there and move with it. We learn from the past because history has a way of repeating itself.

Change is constant. We will have to adjust to the technological advancement of the business, but we cannot lose sight of the basics we learned early – providing quality products and good service, having great people working for us, and taking excellent care of our customers. That is truly what the auto industry is all about. It has been in the past; it is at present; and it will be in the future.

Irma Elder refers to herself as a "truly multi-cultural person." Born in Xicotencalt, Mexico, she moved with her family to Florida as a teen, speaking only a few words of English. While on vacation, she met James Elder, and in 1963 they were married and moved to Michigan. They opened Troy Ford in April 1967, with Mr. Elder running the business and Mrs. Elder at home raising their three children. In November 1983 James Elder died suddenly, leaving his wife to take over the reins of the business. She became a trailblazer of sorts, the first woman to own a Ford dealership in the greater Detroit area.

Since that time, the dealership has undergone many changes, the most notable being its name change to Elder Ford to keep it more closely associated with the family name. Today, the Elder Automotive Group has grown to encompass not only Elder Ford, but also Jaguar of Troy (the number one Jaguar dealership in the world in volume of automotive sales), Saab of Troy (the number one Saab dealership in the United States in volume of automotive sales), Aston Martin of Troy, Signature Ford-Lincoln-Mercury-Jeep of Owosso, Signature Ford of Perry, Jaguar of Tampa, Florida, and Aston Martin of Tampa, Florida.

Mrs. Elder's success is evident not only in the impressive growth of her companies, but also in the recognition she continues to receive. Elder Automotive Group consistently ranks in the top ten of Hispanic Business Magazine's top 500 Hispanic-owned corporations (the only female-owned corporation in the top ten). In addition, Elder is one of the highest-ranking women in Working Woman magazine's top 500 Women in the country.

Irma Elder has received an abundant amount of civic awards and is in constant demand as a speaker, particularly to women's groups. She feels a great responsibility to the women of today's society and works tirelessly to convey her positive message to them.

Mrs. Elder's numerous board activities cover a broad spectrum of interests and purposes. She serves as a board member with groups as diverse as the Chicago Branch of the Federal Reserve Board, Lear Corporation, and the more local Northwood University and Oakland Family Services. The magnitude of her involvement in business and community activities make Irma Elder one of the country's most visible and dynamic community leaders.

FLEXIBILITY IN THE FACE OF CHANGE

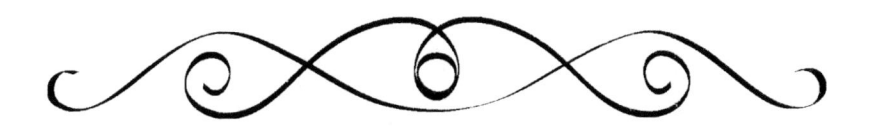

Don Walker

Intier Automotive, Magna's Interiors Company

President and Chief Executive Officer

The Shape of the Industry Today

It's a very exciting time to be in the automotive industry. While change and evolution are part of every industry, the last few years have seen the automotive industry undergo tremendous changes, specifically in automotive manufacturer (what we commonly refer to as "OEM") consolidation. In the face of these changes, suppliers have a choice: Either sit back and react, or exhibit flexibility and proactively plan and take action to maximize these opportunities. The Chinese term for "crisis" is a combination of the words "opportunity" and "threat." It is with this balanced mindset that we must be flexible enough to face the challenges ahead and turn them into opportunities.

A brief look into the recent past will help set the stage for what the future holds. In the early 1990s, it was common for industry analysts and commentators to talk about how the automotive industry was on the verge of a great period of consolidation. By the middle 1990s, it hadn't happened, and many people thought the theories were unfounded. By the end of the decade, however, it was clear the prognosticators had been correct – it had just taken a bit longer than expected. As we settle in to the new millennium, it's very clear that the automotive industry has experienced a huge amount of consolidation among the OEMs.

The result of this consolidation has been a shift to larger and even more global customers. This shift has fundamentally altered the way we do business and the requirements inherent in doing this business. In many instances, these customers require a more consistent approach to conducting business across the various regions of the world. The challenge for suppliers comes not only in geography, but also in the execution of product plans. The development of the large platforms that cross several vehicle segments and lines and are manufactured in several continents poses additional challenges to the industry.

To illustrate the extent of OEM consolidation, consider the automotive manufacturers that once operated independently, but are now controlled by or unified with another manufacturer: Fiat, Saab, Isuzu, and Suzuki are now with General Motors; Renault and Nissan have joined forces, as have Daimler-Benz and Chrysler, which then added Mitsubishi; Ford has added Volvo, Jaguar, Land Rover, and Aston Martin; and Volkswagen/Audi have Skoda and Seat.

The auto world has come together to form essentially six major OEM groups. The automotive companies listed above, with the addition of Toyota, account for the majority of world auto production. Only BMW, Honda, and PSA remain as independents, although the Korean OEMs are showing rapid growth. Even the icon of the auto industry, Rolls Royce, has been acquired and divided. BMW now owns the Rolls Royce name, and VW now owns Bentley and the traditional manufacturing facility in Crewe, England.

If we accept that the unification of several OEMs has changed our world, what does it mean to us as automotive suppliers? Consolidation has resulted in several new challenges and opportunities. While it's helpful to present these challenges as separate sections for the sake of discussion, understand that these challenges are often tied together, with inter-related causes and effects:

- Globalization continues to evolve.
- The Tier One supplier base has been reshaped, with fewer, bigger Tier Ones taking on more responsibility.
- The voice of the consumer takes on greater importance to Tier Ones.
- Cost pressures continue and are intensified for the "new generation" Tier Ones.
- Maximizing shareholder value becomes a greater challenge.

Globalization in Flux

Globalization has been with us for about 20 years, but it's constantly being redefined. Not long ago, globalization primarily meant having facilities and/or offices in several countries around the world to support local supply. It was common to think "We're in North America, Europe, and Japan – we're global." While it'll always be important to maintain operations in the areas of the world where our customers are located, globalization now means something more: It refers to the "commonization" of vehicle platforms (and in some instances systems and modules), that is, producing several vehicle models for several global markets from a single platform with a single engineering source.

The idea itself isn't new, but the extent to which it's happening certainly is. By the late 1990s, only five vehicle platforms generated total volumes of 1 million or more. Companies such as Honda – with the Civic, Integra, RSX, Stream, and Acura EL – and General Motors – with their full size pickup truck sharing the same platform as the Tahoe, Yukon, and Suburban – were the benchmarks at that time for shared platforms.

Other companies have caught on quickly. Where once there were only five, by 2005 there will be approximately 16 global platforms with volumes of 1 million units or more. A fine example of today's globalization is happening at Volkswagen, where the Golf, Jetta, Seat Toledo, Skoda

Octavia, Audi A3, and Audi TT are all produced from a single platform.

Tier Ones: Fewer, Bigger, Bolder

With the redefining of globalization, OEMs have chosen to place more responsibility on their Tier One suppliers. This, in turn, forces the suppliers to increase their internal infrastructure. Obviously, not every company will be able to do this, which essentially means only the strong will survive. With fewer, bigger Tier Ones, the competition increases as it really comes down to who can adapt the fastest, as well as handle the financial impact of these increased responsibilities.

The Tier One suppliers that thrive will have the capability to handle these additional global challenges and the management skills to take on project responsibilities ranging from single components to completely integrated systems. For example, one customer may require only an instrument panel for a single vehicle line, while another will ask you to serve as the lead integrator of the entire interior. As OEMs strive to shorten vehicle-development cycles and bring dynamic products to market more quickly, suppliers must understand the modular approach to building today's vehicles and be prepared to take on additional responsibilities in benchmarking, engineering, development of new technologies, testing, and design.

While it presents challenges, this shift in responsibility has also opened new opportunities for the supply base to have more input and control over the design and manufacture of the products. Concurrently, it enables the car companies to have the best products and designs at the best prices.

The buying public's desire for more content in their cars challenges suppliers to be innovative and adaptive to the engineering requirements needed to support this additional content. Suppliers today must focus on their core competencies and form strategic partnerships to support activities outside their core. Partnerships make sense when they allow you to support innovative vehicle content, deliver value to your customer, and bring flexibility to your business.

In addition to partnerships, enhanced engineering skills are needed for core in-house capabilities to remain unique and innovative. It's important for suppliers and OEMs to attract and retain top engineering talent, as well as to get involved on a local level with students to open their eyes a bit to the excitement and promise of careers in engineering.

Another important skill of the bolder, more flexible Tier One is the ability to control and manage our own supplier network. Our responsibility now often includes managing the supply chain for material, assembly with line-side-friendly components, and just-in-time sequencing from Tier Two and beyond suppliers. Technology advances in supply chain management have made it possible to optimize the delivery of goods, services, and information between the suppliers – all with the objective to improve the combined enterprise's competitiveness. All parties have a vested interest in the quality, reliability, and durability of the products we create, and everyone thinks like a business owner who wants to make sure everything is done right, on time, and on budget.

This notion of how we run the business can't be underestimated. Magna International has always been entrepreneurial and agile, and we brought that part of the Magna heritage with us when we started Intier Automotive. It's part of keeping fear out of the organization and urging our people to always give their absolute best effort and use the processes we have in place. If people feel they can't take risks to give their best, then that's a problem. We realize that sometimes strikeouts are necessary on the way to base hits and home runs. It's all part of instilling accountability into the organization. People need to take it upon themselves to thoroughly assess each situation and go forward in making the best decisions possible. As a group, we need to encourage people to reach out and extend themselves as we foster a culture of innovation.

Ultimately, as a supplier, we need to remember our immediate customers are still the vehicle manufacturers, and our ability to satisfy their needs and wants is still most important to us.

Consumer's Voice Speaks Change

There is a constant need for understanding the end consumer, the people who buy our customers' products. With the Internet, we are living in a time of rapid change and mass access to information. Unlike ten years ago, the consumer is able to quickly and conveniently perform side-by-side comparisons of multiple vehicles and features. This access to immediate information has heightened the need to develop more innovative, value-added products in as short a time as possible.

While listening to the voice of the consumer through consumer clinics and conducting extensive market research have always been a critical first step in our development process, we are excited about this added responsibility. It provides the supplier community an opportunity to demonstrate their total capability. Rather than designing according to specifications passed down from the customer, we can now influence the overall nature of the design based on what we've heard from consumers, as well as with our own expertise. While the end consumer may never know they are sitting in an Intier Automotive interior, they will at least begin to recognize the interior environment becoming more and more consistent with their overall wants and needs.

Heightened awareness of features and functions available throughout the industry has also increased the end consumer's wants and needs when it comes to their vehicle. They have more opinions about vehicle performance, riding comfort, and interior design and execution than ever before. In the past, automotive manufacturers solicited these opinions and used them to assist in the development of their initial vehicle outline or marketing plan. With greater pressures to bring vehicles to market faster and the number of vehicle options increasing, they are now placing the responsibility for assessing the needs of the end consumer on the shoulders of their suppliers.

New Cost Pressures

Consolidation at the OEM level has resulted in fewer manufacturers controlling larger pieces of business, which has magnified cost pressures to suppliers. Additionally, the need for more infrastructure at the supplier level and overcapacity within the industry have resulted in new cost pressures.

As suppliers take on more responsibilities and a larger role in the design and manufacturing process, they need more infrastructure. This includes new facilities with new people and equipment, as well as the tools and resources needed to conduct market research, benchmarking studies, and competitive analysis. These are all costs that many companies did not have several years ago. The issue of overcapacity, coupled with tremendous pressures in the marketplace — people want higher quality vehicles with more options at better prices — has resulted in an unrelenting price squeeze. Overcapacity has forced the OEMs to be more competitive. The primary example right now is with sport-utility vehicles. In 1983, when nobody had heard the term "SUV," buyers who wanted a four-door, four-wheel-drive, multi-purpose vehicle could choose from a group of one: the Jeep Cherokee. In 2002, because of the overwhelming popularity of sport-utility vehicles, there are no fewer than 50 different models to choose from.

This challenge has truly separated the companies that have a viable strategy from those that do not. The key to our strategy has been our strong commitment to engineering and new product development. This enables us to remain competitive and provide the best and most innovative products to our customers and the end consumer.

Another main thrust within our strategy has been to drive waste out of the system and find a balance between growth and cost. We know that to be innovative we must spend money, yet to remain competitive we must find ways to drive cost out. That results in a real premium on efficient execution. Efficiency becomes the goal in every controllable facet – manufacturing, engineering, program management, supplier management, and our suppliers. Continual cost pressure over the years made it even more necessary to become efficient. Every area of the organization must be examined for inefficiency and revised accordingly to be as lean and productive as possible.

Maximizing Shareholder Value

Closely related to the overcapacity issue is the challenge of maximizing shareholder value. Overcapacity drives inefficiencies and poor returns on the investment of capital, which means that everyone is less profitable. Long-term enhancement of profitability can be done only through streamlining our product development process and improving the performance of our operations.

Balancing the interests of stockholders with those of customers is another challenge. We approach this challenge with the philosophy that if we run the business well, everyone will be happy in the end. We do not do anything short-term to please the customer, because it will bring disappointment in the long term. The long term is ultimately important, and pleasing both constituencies requires that we keep employees motivated and keep customers happy by using an efficient model. This will stimulate growth and profits, which will drive earnings up – and this will please the shareholders.

Flexibility: The Platform for Success

Given the changes in the marketplace, it is necessary to position your company to thrive on this change, rather than be threatened by it. We have organized our company to be flexible and agile. We have a decentralized business structure with autonomous business units and people who are responsible for their product areas. Our structure and autonomy give our business managers the opportunity to act quickly to take advantage of situations that arise. We also have very little bureaucracy, which leads to a more efficient company. To facilitate this lean and responsive organization, we have initiated many programs that involve our employees and management in profit-sharing. This helps to motivate our people and align their goals to the goals and success of the organization as a whole.

Within our organization we try to foster an environment where a manager has the autonomy and flexibility to make good and timely decisions. Given this environment, we choose and equip our managers with strong technical knowledge, which we believe is critical to execute at the highest levels. We also monitor and track the quality of the decisions made and frequently assess the results achieved. Based on these assessments, it is easy to see whether a manager is executing well because key metrics such as sales, employee morale, and profitability will increase. I cannot emphasize enough that the success of a company depends on the performance of these managers.

When positioning a company to succeed, it is necessary to make sure you have the proper organization and compensation structure that will keep employees motivated while keeping bureaucracy to a minimum. Give everyone a piece of the business, so everyone has a vested interest in the operation and outcome of the business. To ensure that employees feel a part of the business, we get employee feedback via annual surveys, fairness committees, and a hotline for complaints. We also have profit-sharing that is partially cash and partially stock. The shares in the company are there for the long haul. We want our employees to feel like owners of the company.

Internally, I tell people to focus on putting those with technical expertise in the decision-making positions. If the role is operational or engineering, we look for someone with a technical background, who is analytical with a good business sense. This person must be fair but tough. In different fields there will be different areas of expertise required, but that technical knowledge must be there. In general, managers must be aggressive, confident, moral, and hard-working. Those are the desired traits.

Management Style: The Entrepreneurial Way

The flexibility to change is necessary not only in our organization, but my own management style is also changing to accommodate what's taking place in the industry. Ultimately, management style evolves as a result of the people you work with, and by someone mentoring you or showing you how things operate or should operate. I try to support and foster consensus with the people who should be involved in making the decisions. I then try to prioritize what needs to be done and complete the high-priority tasks before moving on to the rest of the list. It is important to spend the most time where that time will reap the largest return for your efforts. The key here is prioritizing. I try to identify what issues will have the largest impact on the business, whether through future product development, sales growth, structure of the company, or the right people in the right job, and then focus on it. It is important to pick out of the forest the trees that will affect the whole.

A huge challenge of such a manager is to harness employees' talents so that the machine of the company functions smoothly and efficiently. This happens autonomously. We let people who are aligned with product lines decide where they spend their time and money, on innovation or research. We want people who are committed long-term to specific business units. We will then tie them to the success of that unit. We want them to be committed seven years down the road, so that their level of motivation remains high.

Being a leader in the automotive industry takes technical expertise and an ability to solve problems. It also takes the willingness to work hard and demand the best from those around you. At the senior level you must be entrepreneurial. The industry is very dynamic, so the leaders of the company must be willing to look at new ways to do things and be ready to adjust to changes in the marketplace. As a leader, the worst thing possible is to fail a business by poor decision-making. It is difficult for a manager to see the livelihood of his or her employees suffering due to a wrong decision. People depend on managers for their livelihood, and this puts things in focus.

Foreign Markets: Opportunities for Growth

Internal success extends to external success, and one factor of external success is growth. When you enter a new foreign market, you need to understand the culture, first and foremost. You must understand this when entering the market and when dealing with customers and employees. You must build a management team that understands the values and structure of the company so that they can meld into the company, keep the customers happy by keeping the quality standards in place, and continuously motivate employees. This team must do these things to make the right decisions in that local market.

One of the challenges of becoming global is understanding the local legal and commercial risks when operating in foreign markets. The only way to resolve this is by choosing the people who can deal correctly with the problems unique to that country and area of the market. Most of the global growth for the automotive industry will likely shift to some brand-new markets. Moving into new markets inherently contains the most risk. However, the areas that will grow the most must have the currency and legal systems to support an industry.

Envision Success

When positioning for success, setting goals is a critical first step. Outlining a plan is necessary, and the overall execution of the plan is most important. Once priorities are set and a strategy is put in place for the future, success will be determined by the execution of the strategy. If you fail to plan, you plan to fail, especially in this industry that is so technically driven. Many entrepreneurs who develop new companies and new products are not technically apt, but are the idea guys. There are creative people, motivators, and technical experts, and a successful business needs all of these in the right balance.

To be successful, a company must understand the future, and especially the future growth areas of the industry. As car companies continue to focus on their core business, there is good opportunity for suppliers to introduce innovative new products in the interior, powertrain, and driveline areas. However, the largest opportunity is in improving existing products and processes. The Internet will have a huge impact on logistics, information flow and reduced inventories. Non-value-added activities, whether in processing paper or doing things that could be done more efficiently, will be eliminated. As far as the vehicle itself is concerned, there is a push for lightweight materials to replace conventional steel, but there is no major product area that will disappear in the near future. Electronics will take a larger role in the functionality of vehicles.

Because of the importance of understanding industry trends, one of the most critical jobs of a company leader is product strategy. You also have to drive an innovative culture, have the right structure, pick the right people, set the priorities, and maintain the flexibility and agility to turn change into opportunities. To stay on top of the industry, I would say the best thing to do is to be aware of what is going on in the industry and pick the right people. One person can do only so much, so an efficient team must be put in place. The golden rule of business in the automotive industry is making the right product at the right price – and that takes good innovation, good product engineering, good manufacturing, and having the agility to put the right people in the right place at the right time.

Don Walker is president and chief executive officer of Intier Automotive, a global, full-service supplier and integrator of automotive interior and closure components, systems, and modules.

Mr. Walker began his began his career in the petroleum industry in 1976 as an engineering student. He worked at

General Motors from 1980 to 1987 in various engineering and manufacturing positions, including superintendent, involved in the launch of a new vehicle assembly plant. He joined Magna in 1987, initially responsible for various engineering and joint venture projects. In 1991 he was appointed executive vice president and chief operating officer. In 1992 he became president, and in 1994 became president, chief executive officer, and a member of the board of directors.

In February 2001, Magna's board of directors approved a corporate reorganization in accordance with Magna's spin-off policy. As part of this restructuring, in August 2001 Magna spun off its interiors group, comprising the operations of Magna's Atoma Closure Systems Group, Magna Seating Systems Group, and Magna Interior Systems Group, as a publicly traded corporation. Accordingly, Mr. Walker was named president and chief executive officer of Intier Automotive, Inc. He also remains a member of the Magna board of directors and serves as chairman of Magna's Executive Strategy Committee.

Mr. Walker is a member of the Yves Landry Advisory Foundation, which promotes the value of technical education in the school system and reform of the apprenticeship program. He is a past chairman of the Automotive Parts Manufacturers Association (APMA) and co-chair of the Automotive Advisory Committee to the Federal Government of Canada. In 2000 Mr. Walker became a member of the Board of Covisint, an e-business automotive exchange that allows customers and suppliers to bid, source, and purchase components on the Web. In 1999 he received the Professional Engineers of Ontario Gold Medal Award. He is a member of Top 40 Under 40 Awards in Canada.

Mr. Walker graduated from the University of Waterloo with a BA Sc. Mechanical Engineering degree in 1980.

THE IMPORTANCE OF KNOWING THE BUSINESS

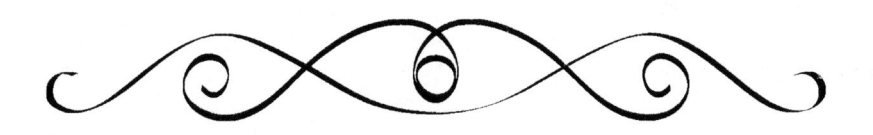

Vic Edelbrock

Edelbrock Corporation,
Edelbrock Foundry Corporation

Chairman, President, Chief Executive Officer

Hands-on Management

Over the years, I've developed an uncanny feel for what's going on in my company. That's probably what most people would say when asked about my management style. I can smell things, and when there's a problem I go to it and say, "Hey, there's a problem right there; let's get it fixed." That's just from being around and having a real feel for my company and the things that are happening all the time. Also, I have the kind of personality that can create a positive atmosphere when I'm here in the building – people really want to work for me and to do a good job.

I work closely with our vice presidents of manufacturing and R&D – helping them manage their problems and giving them direction regarding where I think we should go. In this business you don't have time to sit back; you have to be fairly prompt because if you aren't, that customer is going to take those dollars and buy something else. When we make product on the engineering side, we have to do it in a timely manner and keep moving. That's one thing I stay on top of. When it goes over to manufacturing, we have to make sure we produce it in a timely manner. If it doesn't get to shipping, then it doesn't get to our customers, and then they can't sell it. So I stay very close to that. I'm a hands-on guy here; I'll sweep the floor if I have to.

Being hands-on is going from department to department and being able to see things and correct them – getting with the people involved and saying, "This is something I think we're off on and want to change," or "We don't have this product on order, and we should. Let's get it on order from our foundry because we're going to run out." It's being involved on a day-to-day basis – more than just sitting in my office and talking to my VPs. I'm going out there to make things move more quickly and smoothly and to prevent hiccups later. I also have to communicate very well with the people around me, under me, and within the company structure so they know what's going on.

My knowledge of the company and business is one of my most important characteristics as CEO. I have a good feel for the company – that's probably the number one thing.

My personality, keeping people excited, whether they're my employees or our customers, is number two. The ability to run a company – to watch the cash and balances and make sure we don't run out of money – is number three. Even though I have good people to keep on top of the money, it doesn't stop there. I have to be involved with that and know where we're going so we don't have a catastrophe or a real problem down the line.

Encouraging Innovation and Generating Excitement

To encourage innovation among my employees, I point out that the more innovative they are, the more we sell, the more profit we make, and the more money they make. We're on a bonus basis here, and we look at that every year. It's a matter of the growth of the company, the profit of the company – from R&D creating new products to manufacturing making quality products at the lowest possible cost, right on through to advertising and sales – the whole organization. Everybody's involved to make this company grow and have a solid bottom line, so we share in the results. Also, we like to promote from within whenever possible, and we've been quite successful in doing that. We just hired a person for manufacturing from the outside, but we had to do that because we didn't have anybody to bring up from within. In most cases we try to educate our people to the point where they can promote themselves if they want to move through the company.

To generate enthusiasm among my employees, I start by going around and learning as many names as I can. We have 600 people, so I don't know all their names, but I try. I'm a part of the team, and I let them know that. I'm very strong on it. Going around and with a fresh look on your face and saying, "How are you? Have a good morning (or evening or weekend)" is the easiest thing you can do: It doesn't cost you a thing to be nice to your employees.

To generate the excitement and buzz around our products with our customers, we follow the same philosophy we've had since my father started this company back before World War II – to always make what you would have run on your own car, and to be pleased with it. That way, if you ever have a problem, you can look the guy straight in the eye and say, "Hey, you've got a problem here? This works and it works well. Let's get together and find the problem so you can be as happy as I am with our product." By making a product that I know works, I can look people straight in the eye and know I have a product that does the job they want it to do. Customer service is extremely important in the segment of the industry we're in.

Our business is an exciting segment of the auto industry because we deal with engines – we deal with performance cars, and we make them run better. The excitement is in making our products do what we expect them to do and selling that excitement. I was recently at Cobo Hall in Detroit, at one of the biggest car shows in the country. They run almost 200,000 people through this show in three days. They have 800 cars on display. It's quite an event. Being there and talking to our customers and signing posters and autographs and hearing the enthusiasm they have for our product really builds the excitement factor. I have a lot of that happening everywhere I go. People come up and thank me for making our product. That's the

The Automotive Industry

excitement that this industry generates – we're more than just an automotive manufacturing-type business.

Where we are, in the aftermarket, the most challenging thing we encounter is coming up with something that performs and works, and then telling the customer about it and pulling it through. By "pulling it through," I mean we have to pre-sell the customer so he will go in and say, "This is what I want. This works." And then we go from there. That is our challenge – to keep new products coming out, to keep our growth, and to make sure the products work and that we advertise properly, pulling that product through. I'm also involved with advertising as part of sales. If we don't get a customer who goes out and says, "I want an Edelbrock such and such," then we have not done our job in pulling it through. We might sell the warehouse a complete line of product, but if we don't pull it through to the consumer, then we haven't done our job, and that can eventually come back on us. That's what our big challenge is.

Five-year-old cars are the primary peak of our business. That gives us time to see what the Big Three are doing, and we watch them very closely. We know people there, and we do business with GM and Ford through their motor support program, keeping abreast of their activities. We watch what they're doing and how they're doing it, and when something new comes out, we look at what we're going to do. It may take us two or three years to get into the particular thing we need to do, but then we're ready for it. We have to watch very closely. We're not privy to info on what Ford, GM, and Chrysler will do in the next two or three years. We don't see that, and there's no way we can unless we're involved in making parts for that particular vehicle. We have to wait for it to happen, then go from there.

If you want your company to become a leader in this industry, you have to come up with a good product line – new products every year that work. It's just as simple as that. In this business you can't make your name and then rest on your laurels or sit on your hands. You have to keep moving all the time, making new products, publicizing them the best possible way, always pre-selling them – and keep that going continuously.

Measuring Success and Looking to the Future

We measure success based on our growth, on our product, on the projections of that growth (as much as we can), and on what we hear out there. If you build a good reputation, people notice, and when you make something, they say, "It has to be good – it has to be right, or they wouldn't make it." Stock price is another measure of success. We have to have the proper management here to do our job, but then we don't want to be top-heavy, either, so that's always something that you have to contend with. We work very hard at that – at being maybe a little lean – and we all get the work done to keep the profits up. Profits make our stock do what it wants to do, enabling our people to receive higher bonuses.

At our level, we have to watch very closely what's being made and stay on top of the industry. We have to be able to react and rapidly fill those niche markets we find so that we don't lose them or the customer. We have to continue to make product and get it on the shelf in a timely manner. That is a key factor.

Looking to the future, we have to watch what the Big Three do. We have to watch the evolution of the automobile and which way it's going to go. As these cars become more sophisticated, with more complex electronics, we have to make sure there is something there we can work into our system. Fortunately, our market is about five years behind, giving us a little time to look at what's being made. We can look at it closely, buy a car, drive it, and then find out how and in what areas we can help it.

Fortunately, in this business, many people tend to go back to older cars because they don't want to get involved with the newer cars and all their changes. There's a great deal of family involvement in our particular part of the business. A father who was a performance guy in his day and who has kids that are approaching driving age can build a street rod or a street machine or something his kids can be involved with in the wintertime. They can go to the many car shows and events held during the spring, summer, and fall. We also work with older cars, so we make sure we have the right product and fill all available niches.

We have two segments. We have the new car segment, and there's some business there, but usually a car rolls around to us when it's about five years old or when it goes to its second owner. Then we have the old hobby-type cars – from street rods that go back to 1949 and muscle cars that go from 1950 on up as a center target for our business and our growth.

Business Advice

The best advice I've received is to always make things you would use yourself on your own vehicles and would be very pleased with. As I mentioned earlier, when a customer comes to you and says a product doesn't work, you need to be able to look him in the eye and say, "It does work. Let's just get to the bottom of it and find out what the problem is." This statement came from my father. It's been very important to me, and I have never really forgotten it. I had a lot of friends in the business who came and told me things and gave me advice when my father passed away in 1962. I have one friend now who told me to make a certain product for a certain engine. At first I said no, but three days later I changed my mind, and that probably really turned this company around. That one product started us on our growth cycle.

I've received other valuable advice, as well: Be fair with people. Be up-front with people, and look them straight in the eye. It's very beneficial to whatever you do.

The advice I always give is to communicate. Communicate with everybody at the same level. I think you really have to keep on top of good communication because it's an easy thing to slip away from.

I also always tell people to be sure they make the best product possible and that they don't have any product on the market that isn't worthy of carrying their name. You have to keep that name up at the top of the pile – keep the respect of your customer. When they buy your product,

The Automotive Industry

they know they're getting the best, and it will do what you tell them it does.

Vic Edelbrock has witnessed the unprecedented growth of the automotive aftermarket industry from its very beginnings. His father, Vic Edelbrock Sr., was a pioneer in the industry. He started Edelbrock Equipment Co. in 1938 and became known as an expert in performance. Vic Edelbrock, Jr., assumed the position of chairman of the board, president, and chief executive officer of Edelbrock Corporation in 1962, when his father passed away. He has built Edelbrock into a multi-million dollar corporation by continuing the tradition of high-quality parts and proven performance.

Mr. Edelbrock has also been actively involved in the industry. He was president of the Specialty Equipment Marketing Association (SEMA) from 1970 to 1974 and served on the SEMA Board of Directors from 1967 to 1989. His list of awards includes being inducted into the SEMA Hall of Fame and the Street Rod Equipment Alliance (SREA) Hall of Fame and being named Performance

65

Warehouse Association (PWA) Person of the Year in 1982 and 1987. Mr. Edelbrock was a regional finalist in the 1995 Entrepreneur of the Year awards competition sponsored by Ernst & Young.

In 1988 Mr. Edelbrock opened Edelbrock Foundry Corp., an aluminum green sand foundry. This facility has been called the most modern aluminum foundry west of the Mississippi. The Edelbrock Foundry casts all aluminum parts for Edelbrock, as well as for several other companies.

A native of Southern California, Mr. Edelbrock attended the University of Southern California, where he has been an active alumnus since graduation in 1958. He resides in Rolling Hills, California.

MANAGING OPPORTUNITIES IN THE AUTO INDUSTRY

Linda Hasenfratz

Linamar Corporation

Chief Executive Officer and President

Trends in the Automotive Industry

Technological developments are changing the face of the automotive supply industry while creating new opportunities for business at the same time. For example, there is a tremendous opportunity for growth in precision machining and assembly. From a dollar perspective, there is more than $100 billion worth of materials and work in precision machining and assembly in the highly engineered areas of the vehicle *(e.g.,* brakes, engine, steering, suspension, transmission, and driveline), where we are focused at Linamar Corporation. The move toward more modularity is creating new competition, as we all aspire toward the same module.

The globalization and standardization of engine and transmission platforms that are evolving in some places will cover several different manufacturers and create more opportunities in terms of the volume of production. That means there will be more opportunities, but obviously they will be available for fewer companies because there will no longer be a need to divide parts among several different suppliers.

Our long-term goal is to grow within the brake, engine, steering, transmission, and driveline systems, starting with machined components and evolving to assemblies, modules, and eventually full systems. Fortunately, there is a huge opportunity for growth in those parts because although the OEMs (original equipment manufacturers) do most of that work themselves, they have established a pattern of outsourcing most of the manufacturing-type work they do. Clearly our goals are aligned, which is a good opportunity for growth. I would like to see the OEMs completely outsource all the transmission, engine, brake, steering, and driveline systems, of course. This will take a long time because those parts make up the heart of the vehicle. If your engine doesn't work, you will be a lot more dissatisfied than if your seatbelt sticks or if your seat doesn't pull forward easily. It's more difficult to give up those important components or modules because of their critical nature to vehicle performance. It will require successes on the part of suppliers to really accelerate that process.

I think foreign companies will follow the same pattern of outsourcing. We haven't seen a great deal of it until now because the volumes haven't been at a level in North America that would be economical for them to buy here when they're making so much higher volume in Asia. It's just so much cheaper to use their Asian source for an extra 100,000 units than to try to use a company in North America. As they continue to pick up market share in North America and increase their volume of production here, I think it will make the North American supply base much more competitive.

Globalized industry management brings a new set of challenges. If your company has locations outside of your home country, you really have to understand how business works in those foreign countries. That involves being sensitive to the cultural differences of that country. Many companies underestimate the cultural factor when doing business elsewhere. For example, it is not a "slam dunk" when you tell someone what you expect from them. They may interpret your request differently, depending on the language spoken. It is certainly a challenge from a communication perspective in both language and distance. How do you interact with that management group often enough to know and understand what's going on and to be able to support them? Using face-to-face meetings on a regular basis is a start, but it will also be necessary to use the Internet, e-mail, teleconferencing, and videoconferencing.

Environmental compliance will continue to be an important issue in the future. There has been significant progress in environmentally friendly technology. Hybrid engines, electric cars, fuel cells, and other new innovations are products of a desire to create a cleaner-burning engine that provides sufficient power for the vehicle. From an environmental standpoint, regulations will only get more stringent, so we should all be aware of the necessity to make those developmental changes. That means companies should not simply meet the current minimum required standard; innovations that go beyond the requirement will be more successful and competitive. For example, not all automakers are demanding ISO14000 registration for environmental compliance, but we are using that standard as a target at all of our plants, because we believe that one day it will be expected.

A common misconception is that suppliers should be lumped into the cyclical patterns of the auto industry; everyone goes up and down, suppliers and automakers alike. However, if there is growth in one segment of the business, you may not have the big drops in sales and earnings you might see on the OEM level because you will continue to gain market share as more of that work comes out. That lumping of suppliers and manufacturers is a misconception because suppliers can still grow during a downturn, or at least minimize their lack of growth. Our ability to maintain a strong business during any economy will allow us to continue to grow and develop useful technology for the future.

Consolidation of the Supply Base

Fewer people are involved in supplying auto parts than there were 20 years ago. Today the emphasis is on design-and-build, rather than simply building a car based on specifications. As a result, the culture and capabilities of the supply base have changed. The suppliers are more involved in engineering and product development work than ever before. Suppliers spend a great deal of time and money to develop and build to the level required by the automotive industry. From a supplier perspective, shrinking the supply base allows creation of enough critical mass to be able to take on larger projects that are being spun out by the OEM, which is positive for business.

Another advantage of the consolidation of the supply base is that it increases efficiency. Instead of buying from several smaller shops, auto manufacturers can consolidate their purchases with two or three key suppliers for a particular type of product. From an OEM perspective, universal platforms will provide greater opportunities for the supply base; instead of five 200,000-unit platforms, there will be just one 1,000,000-unit platform. Not only is the opportunity large from a sales and earnings perspective, but it is also gives you more bang for your buck. For example, if you have a program making a million units per year, and you can save a dollar per unit, that's a million dollars you've saved. From an OEM perspective, it puts more and more power into fewer and fewer hands, so it puts the burden on suppliers to prove their competitiveness. You need to manage the opportunity.

We will have to mobilize production as we start on an upturn in business. That's always a positive thing, but it can be difficult to get everybody back on an up-kick. There has been a lot of fallout from the recent downturn. Suppliers have been hurt quite badly financially; some will survive and some will not. Having fewer suppliers will obviously change the face of business, creating opportunities for the survivors to take on some of those contracts from the companies that didn't make it. Companies need to face this challenge with innovation; they cannot just produce bulk amounts, as size is not enough to survive. You need to be innovative, not just in the products, but also in the process;

you need to maintain the level of innovation and ingenuity you see at a small company while becoming the larger company you need to be.

The Supplier-Manufacturer Relationship

Over the past five to seven years, the automakers learned a great deal about their suppliers through the implementation of quality tracking systems. OEMs are able to compare the costs, quality, and the overall effect of a particular supplier on their business. There is definitely a greater awareness of the importance of supplier relationships.

From the supplier perspective, there needs to be an understanding of the client's expectations and problems. If you know the client's problems, you can be better prepared to solve them. It is important to establish relationships on all levels within both organizations. Your top people should be meeting with their top people so that they are aware of you, your capabilities, and how you've changed. Middle management should be meeting from both sides, while people from your shop floors should be visiting their shop floors. Interaction at all levels will create very clear understanding of your customer's expectations. If you perform to their expectations and they fully understand your capabilities and are taking advantage of them, then you will have a successful relationship. If you are preempting their problems and issues by developing new products and processes that will help address them before they even acknowledge the issues, then you will obviously win business with them. If communication channels are strong, you will be helping each other constantly, and that is a win-win situation.

Clients such as General Motors, Ford, and Daimler-Chrysler have a great deal of power in their hands. They are all huge players in a rather small market, which puts suppliers on the short end of the negotiating stick. With many suppliers but few manufacturers, you as a supplier are not in a position of strength. As both suppliers and modularity continue to grow, however, it will start to equalize the playing field. If you are building a huge module within a vehicle, as some suppliers are doing now, you will certainly have more leverage. In that situation, the customer is married to the supplier in a way that is different than if the customer were buying something that is essentially a commodity that could easily be purchased from another supplier. This builds a healthier relationship; both parties need to win, so they will both be willing to make changes to try to benefit both of them.

Effective Leadership in the Auto Industry

The president of the company needs to create a vision and a strategy and communicate them to employees so that everyone understands them and projects a consistent image of the company. That image is what attracts customers, employees, and shareholders to the company. I think that's the primary job of any business leader – to project that image positively and accurately so that you get the employees you want, the customers you need, and the shareholders you need. You must communicate a clear vision, clear expectations, and a clear direction for the company, quantify your long-term and short-term goals, and follow up to ensure goals and expectations are met. It is then more likely that people working for you will make the same decisions you would make. In a way, when your employees fully appreciate and comprehend that vision, they become empowered in the decision-making process. They know which way you want to go, so they don't have to ask you beforehand.

It is important to give people some rope, but you also need to hold them accountable. If they don't do a good job, you have to address the problem. Great vision and goals don't mean much if they are not met and if there are no consequences for not meeting them. Many managers have difficulty dealing with the people who aren't working well.

The key to success in any business is having the right people in the right jobs. Finding, attracting, and retaining top-level talent is completely critical to any company's success. If you do a good enough job of making the employees equally as important as customers and shareholders, then you have succeeded as a leader. When you have the right people, others will come to you. You won't have to work to attract people because they'll line up at your door. That, to me is a key element in running a business. You need to encourage your employees to work hard and be innovative by rewarding them when they do a good job. If you want to create an idea culture, then you reward the people who come up with ideas – you reward people who succeed and celebrate their success. Put them up on a stage to tell everyone else about it, so everyone can learn from their success and make their own improvements.

Our company has a clear set of goals in a variety of areas that we apply across every facility. We rank everybody to see who's doing the best in certain areas and overall. It creates an element of competitiveness and innovation as employees try to achieve recognition as the best. At the same time, we orient ourselves around team-based management and team-based solutions, as opposed to individuality. We recognize that having two or three or four people addressing a problem is more likely to result in a better solution than having one person facing it alone.

To lead effectively, you have to keep up to date on the industry. I read *Automotive News* every week to stay on top of developments, and I spend time with supplier organizations such as the OESA and, in Canada, the APMA, where I can discuss issues with other suppliers. I also like to talk to customers as often as I can, asking them what they're doing and what more we can be doing for them, so that I am aware of people's needs and aware of what's going on in the industry.

Linda Hasenfratz was named chief executive officer of Linamar Corporation on August 12, 2002; she has been president since April 1999. From September 1997 to September 1998 she was chief operating officer of Linamar, a global manufacturer of precision-machined components, assemblies, and castings primarily for the automotive industry.

Ms. Hasenfratz joined Linamar Corporation in July 1990 and embarked on an extensive training program to gain familiarity with all aspects of the business. Between July 1990 and September 1991, positions she held include machine operator, quality assurance technician, engineering technician, production control coordinator, and operations manager.

In September 1991, Ms. Hasenfratz was appointed materials manager of the then new Traxle subsidiary. After this two-year placement, Ms. Hasenfratz assumed responsibility for Traxle's accounting department as administrative manager for ten months. She spent the next five months in the marketing department, completing her exposure to most functions of the business.

In January 1995, Ms. Hasenfratz assumed responsibility for the startup of Comtech Mfg. Ltd. as operations manager. As operations manager for Comtech and later for the Vehcom Manufacturing subsidiary, Ms. Hasenfratz was fully responsible for the day-to-day operations of both facilities, ensuring customer satisfaction, employee satisfaction, and profitability objectives were met. She was named the general manager for both facilities in June 1997.

Ms. Hasenfratz completed an Executive MBA from the Ivey School of Business at the University of Western Ontario in June 1997. In addition, Ms. Hasenfratz holds an Honours Bachelor of Science degree from the same institution. The analytical and strategic planning skills she gained in the MBA program and the practical skills she has gained at Linamar are key factors in her executive development.

LESSONS IN AUTOMOTIVE ENTREPRENEURSHIP

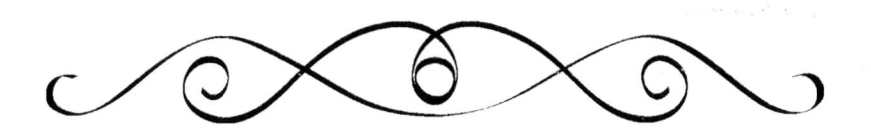

Scott L. Thompson

Group 1 Automotive

Executive Vice President,
Chief Financial Officer, and Treasurer

Entrepreneurial Spirit and Leadership

Automobile retailing is an industry that requires the operators to have a great deal of entrepreneurial spirit. This spirit lends itself to a decentralized operation where the operators are empowered and given the tools to run their business and be successful. I do not think a command-and-control structure works well in automobile retailing; these are very difficult businesses to run.

Today one of my greatest challenges is helping these entrepreneurs who join Group 1 make the transition from successful private entrepreneurs to successful executives and officers in a public company. I must also help them understand the public market – how the rules of the game differ in the public world as opposed to the private world. We spend a lot of time on this education. It is exciting for us, as well as for them. The other challenge is on the finance side, in helping Wall Street investors and portfolio managers understand car dealerships. Often their perception of what goes on in a car dealership is very different from the reality. I have to help them understand the business and the drivers in the business to the point where they are comfortable giving the public companies hundreds of millions of dollars to invest. So it requires education on the human capital side with the entrepreneurs, and on the other side it requires education with the investors.

We have a very open management style at Group 1. We have always put in long hours – we were doing 24/7 before we even knew what that meant. When you put in so many hours, you must be able to have fun at work. We like to maintain a fun, open, and loose environment. Although we are very professional in our public business, behind closed doors, I encourage employees to share any thoughts they might have. I think some of the best new ideas I've ever heard or seen have come from the people who work for me. At the same time, people who work for me have been very good at keeping me from making mistakes. So, in my management style I like to have fun and an open environment, and keep a close personal relationship with the people who work for me.

Having the right human capital in place is critical for success. To attract the right human capital, you must make the work environment someplace they want to work. This is not just from a pay plan standpoint, but also from an empowerment standpoint. You must give them a feeling of trust, as well as the tools they need to succeed. At Group 1, we give people enough rope to run their business; we don't try to micromanage them. We reward success with trophies and awards and sometimes money. Most people are motivated by the work environment, their ability to succeed, and recognition of that ability. I think the easiest part of running a business is creating a game plan, but the human capital – having people actually execute the plan – is the hard part.

The dream employee for Group 1 will bring energy, integrity, enthusiasm, intelligence, and outstanding communication skills to the table. He or she will have to motivate and educate a large number of people, because one person does not make a dealership run. Everyone needs to motivate, focus, and understand the plan and the goals. This is such a people-dependent business that the employee

The Automotive Industry

or group of employees can have a direct effect on financial results.

Beyond just attracting the right kind of people to work for you and with the public, you must give these people the right tools to be successful. If you do this, the financial performance will come, and you will get noticed. Having a solid track record of doing what you said you would do – or perhaps doing better than you said you would do – certainly helps draw attention to a business.

To be a leader in the automotive industry, I believe that above all, it takes integrity. This industry has a reputation for having problems in that area, and if you are going to lead in it, your word and integrity must be your highest priority. During tough times when decisions are critical, you see the integrity in people. It is easy to be ethical when everything is wonderful, but when things are hard, you need people who are grounded and solid in their principles and who know exactly where they stand and will not let current events change their foundation.

High-energy people who are willing to do what it takes to succeed and make the necessary trade-offs are also important to a business. We want those people who know what they want, but are also aware there is a price to be paid and are willing to pay it without complaint.

The most difficult thing to do as a leader is to make decisions about people. An example is a high-performance person who might perform well from a financial point of view, but whose methods for generating that financial performance are unacceptable, possibly from a customer or a risk standpoint. Having to make decisions about what to do in these situations is by far the toughest task. Clearly, when someone just does not perform, the decision is a lot easier. The hard decision is with someone who is performing, but in a way you are not comfortable with.

Your motivation and desire to succeed are what drive you to continue your personal education. This is what you owe your job and your company; otherwise, the industry and technology will pass you by. You must also lead by example. No one will do anything you say unless you do it yourself. To lead your employees, you must provide an example and challenges for them. If they know the challenges will come their way, they will stay current. In the end, you will promote the people who follow this example and succeed in the challenges. It is not really how long you have been at one place, but what you bring to the table and your depth of knowledge.

Keeping Score

When you work in a variety of industries, you find each has its own terminology, buzz words, and economic drivers that are critical in the business. But, when you get right down to it, business is business. The same core principles need to be applied whether you are working in oil and gas or automobile retailing: People are important and need to motivated and trained; you have to have the right capital; you must control the business through budgeting. Actually, some of the tools we have brought to the automobile industry are both capital and operating budgeting, tying compensation to performance against budget (which is very different from historical compensation plans), and keeping guidelines for a minimum return on invested capital – whether for an acquisition, expanding a dealership, or buying a lift. These are all new to this sector, but we've found them to be a common theme in other industries.

I believe the financial end of the business is really the "score-keeping" part of it. If you want to understand how the business and the people in it are performing, you must understand the score-keeping. Having an in-depth background in accounting and finance, as I do, is critical to understanding all of this.

On a corporate level in a public company, you cannot help looking at stock price as a measure of success. Although there are times when the stock numbers are not in sync with your other measures, checking stock price is certainly a starting point because it truly is the market value of your business on any given day.

On an individual basis, we like to see people grow and develop as businesspeople. As I've said before, we really like to take those outstanding businesspeople from the private sector and convert them into outstanding businesspeople in the public world. I came into this industry with no experience and did not have the same appreciation for the people and the human capital of the business. The best advice I got early on was that people really do matter – that's not just a saying.

Embracing Change and Taking Risks

The ability to thrive on change is a corporate culture issue. You must communicate with people every day about the need for change and that change is good. Most people who are successful can deal with change very well. They realize you cannot get comfortable because no matter what you do, change will happen. Only people who get locked into one strategy see the market eventually move past them. In a public company, though, this does not happen, because the public demands performance and a return on capital every quarter, not just one quarter a year. The public sector really forces you into a culture that is willing to change and embraces change.

If you take no risks, you are simply not moving forward. Every day you must take risk. It all comes down to measuring each risk against the reward you would receive from it. My most signature motto is probably, "I do not mind a lot of risk, but there had better be a lot of reward." I think I must say this about nine times a day. We have minimum investment hurdles on returns so that we can quantify what sort of risk we are taking and for what return. Although you have to take risk to get anything done, it has to be prudent, quantifiable, and controllable risk. You must also have a good dialog with a number of people so that you have everybody's thoughts on what the risks and rewards are on whatever issue you are working through. Then, hopefully, you can have the best people execute the plan.

Judging the reward against the risk is part of the quantifiable process of risk-taking that must be agreed on up front. If you are pitching an idea to a sponsor, you must be able to provide a clear and quantifiable picture of your plan, seeing it through to an advantageous end. If you are not willing to commit to a reward up front, then your sponsor will doubt that you have done your homework and will be less likely to commit capital to your idea.

Looking Forward

To see where the industry might be going in the near future, I think you have to gather information from a variety of sources. You must ardently read periodicals, be active in working your network of contacts, look at other retailers, make certain you are close with your investors, and be open to other people's thoughts about where the industry might go. You cannot get locked into the idea that you *know* where the industry is going, because I don't think anyone knows where the future is headed. I think you get in trouble when you assume you know what is going on. There are now quite a lot of new ideas, with the Internet being the most recent example. And in the vehicles themselves, there are changes in technology and content that may change the industry. The way customers want to buy, and their overall shopping experience, are also changing. So you cannot get locked into what might have been successful in the past.

I am constantly excited by our product, just because – for lack of a better phrase – "cars are neat." There is a true American car experience, where your car gets wrapped up in your personality. My father was an engineer by trade, and I worked in a repair shop as a kid, and we used to rebuild cars together. So, for me, product is without question the most exciting aspect of the industry. Another thing that keeps life interesting is the people. The people who work in this industry are highly motivated, very focused, and competitive.

The complexity of the vehicle is one thing I foresee will significantly change the industry. The new technologies and content that are being put into the vehicles are just incredible. It could be air-conditioned seating, heads-up cruise control, Web-based communication technology, such as OnStar – basically gadgets that make the cars so complex that I think it is going to change the dynamic of where you get your vehicle serviced. I think it will be difficult for people who do not specialize in a particular brand to fix a vehicle. That is even hard for us to do right now. I think there's a movement by retailers and manufacturers toward recognizing the importance customer experience has in helping develop a brand. There is a lot of manufacturing capacity in the world, and to a certain degree it is hard to tell the difference between cars because all of them have gotten so much better from a quality standpoint. And with more countries becoming competitive in the industry, a higher level of quality is constantly being introduced. So now I think what we'll see is that people will have to compete more on customer experience. This encompasses how you buy your car, how your car is serviced, and the general relationship between the customer and the salesperson.

Ideally, I would like to create relationships with customers that go beyond just selling them cars. I would like to have a lifetime experience with them, taking care of their transportation needs. New cars are the least profitable for us, so what we need is a customer who will buy a new car and return to us for all of his or her repair needs, then sell the car on trade-in to us for our used car lots. We need that whole cycle with the customer. No business that simply sells a car for $100 over invoice and never sees the customer again will have a high return on their investment.

These businesses generate a lot of cash flow, and the critical thing is to reinvest that cash flow into operations, additional dealerships, and standard operations that give you the ability to drive earnings and revenues, even though the overall market is pointed down. I think that is what we've seen in the past three quarters – automobile retailers have done very well in their earnings and revenue growth, but the manufacturers have struggled.

In the retail side of the automobile business world, we have a much more flexible model. The manufacturer has a lot of union labor and fixed overhead, so when the volumes drop, they have real financial problems. The retailer has a much more variable cost structure, with about 65 percent of the cost structure being variable and most of it pay plans. So it is much easier for the retailer to manage during downturns than it is for the manufacturer. Still, we watch both personnel and inventory costs closely and reduce our inventory to fit whatever the market requires at the time.

The Automotive Industry

We also focus on our non-cyclical businesses, such as parts and service, which are profitable for us in good times as well as in bad, since people tend to keep their cars longer in a bad economy. It is truly the flexibility of our business model that makes it easier to adjust to economic conditions.

Customer experience is the foundation for building a long-lasting automotive company. I have always believed that cost control may get you into the game, but customer experience will keep you there and eventually let you win that game. If you want to be a success in the industry, there are three things you must keep in mind: It is very important to keep your finger on the people; you must pay attention to what they say, how they say it, and have a feel for what they might be thinking. You must also focus on the market – its major trends – and make certain your company is positioned correctly. Finally, you must be aware of the financial health of the company. You have to have the balance sheets, financial resources, and cash flow to implement your strategy and to be here a hundred years from now.

Scott L. Thompson, executive vice president,, chief financial officer, and treasurer, joined Group 1 Automotive as senior vice president in December 1996. He oversees finance, technology, risk management, investor relations, legal, and human resources.

From 1991 to 1996, Mr. Thompson served as executive vice president of Operations and Finance for KSA Industries, Inc., a billion-dollar private enterprise with interests in automotive retailing, energy, and professional sports. Among Mr. Thompson's responsibilities in the KSA group of companies, he served as executive vice president of the Houston Oilers professional football team and as vice president and director of three Houston-area automobile dealerships. Additionally, in connection with his position at KSA Industries, Inc., he served as a director of Adams Resources Energy, Inc., a public oil and gas company. He is a Certified Public Accountant, and from 1980 to 1991, he held various positions with increasing responsibility at a public accounting firm.

EXCITING AND CHALLENGING ELEMENTS OF THE AUTOMOTIVE INDUSTRY

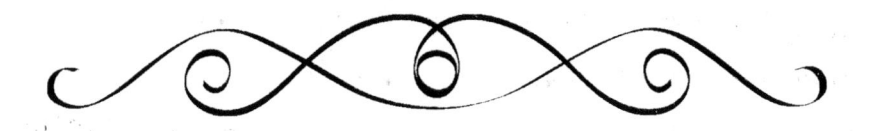

Nancy Lee Gioia

Ford

Vehicle Line Director, Lifestyle Vehicles

Passion for the Product

The ability to make cars, trucks, and SUVs that make a difference in people's lives springs me out of bed every day and drives my overall passion for the industry. The automobile industry is vital to personal mobility. It is responsible for our ability to go where we want when we want. Vehicles have revolutionized our personal lives, changed the urban landscape, and helped us show our individual spirit.

The other thing that makes the auto industry distinct is the emotions the products evoke. For example, people simply bond with their work truck and become passionate about their daily driver. I think about my 2002 Thunderbird and the joy and passion – the total sense of freedom – I have when I'm driving it. To me it is a work of art; it isn't just about getting somewhere – it is how you get there that makes the difference.

Automobiles not only are inspirational and mobilizing, but they also changed our social landscape. I asked my Nana, my great aunt, who lived to be 98, what the two most important inventions in the world are, and she said the first was the telephone, because it drastically changed the ability to communicate, and second was the automobile, because it opened up a whole new realm of living. In each case, long distances were no longer a major barrier. That brings a smile to my face each day at work for obvious reasons as I try to develop the next revolutionary breakthrough in personal mobility that will change the world as we know it.

Challenges for the Auto Industry

With that in mind, let's take a look at some of the issues that are challenging the automotive industry.

One aspect of the industry that I find exciting and rewarding is safety. I look at the events that happen to a vehicle in a crash environment and how automakers seamlessly integrate life-saving systems that all work together and find it simply amazing. The delivery of these systems is something I take personal satisfaction from because the bottom line is that we as an industry are saving lives. Honestly, it is difficult to put into words the rewarding feelings I get when I hear about how a friend's or family member's life was spared in a vehicle I have worked on to make sure it is safe.

For example, Ford is currently working on a V4 four-point safety belt design that offers better control of occupant motion in many types of impacts. This makes me extremely proud. The world of auto racing has known for years that the key to safety success is keeping a person in the seat, but automakers have had considerable trouble placing restraints in passenger vehicles. I honesty hope new technology such as these safety belts proves viable in passenger vehicles because it will represent a breakthrough technology that will certainly safe lives. This, combined with constant education on the importance of the use of safety belts and other features, is critical. These types of inventions will transcend one automaker and affect the entire industry as whole.

Another aspect is the influence the automotive industry has in the community. Whether it is the suppliers, the assembly

The Automotive Industry

plants, the infrastructure, or the sales and services in some format or another, the industry affects everyone. From a person who owns a dealership, the individuals who work in the assembly plants, design engineers, our neighbors next door, aunts, and uncles – they all are interwoven into the world of automobiles. The way automakers do business has a tremendous impact on the community, not just locally but also around the world, and companies such as Ford, Honda, and GM are setting high expectations. How the industry interfaces with the community and defines what is fair, what is equitable, and what is quality is extremely important to the world.

The reason for this is that the automotive business is a passionate one. People view themselves as extensions of the cars and trucks they drive. What they purchase reveals part of their personality and what they care about. It also represents a key to their personal freedom, mobility at their choice. In addition, a vehicle is a very large purchase and is something that is important to people and typically represents a large portion of their income. With that in mind, the whole aspect of the industry's delivery, support, and overall customer satisfaction is critical. For me, being part of this personal connection is a key inspiration.

New technologies present an extremely interesting challenge. The industry goes through times when there are many new opportunities to add the latest and greatest new technologies. Tough decisions have to be made: Do you rush that hot technology into the latest car in the cycle plan as a product itself? Do you look at how it will work in the future? Automakers must keep in mind that some people keep their vehicle for eight to ten years, while others may have their vehicle only two to three years. These time frames of a product life cycle are certainly not unique to the automotive industry, but the mating of many different products (audio/entertainment, tracking/communication systems, vehicle controls, etc.) into one product is. The industry must be constantly vigilant for these opportunities and must strike a good balance between what the customer would like to have immediately and whether or not the technology will endure for the time that many of our customers would like to keep their vehicles. This vigilance doesn't stop with technology.

There is also consolidation and economy of scale occurring in the industry. Economic pressures are growing on a worldwide basis, and the competition continues to expand throughout the industry. For me, as a key player in the industry, these forces make it extremely difficult to come up with different ways of doing things because the risks are so high. It also says we must continue to innovate in what we do and how we do things to remain competitive and meet growing demands.

Whether it is within the Original Equipment Manufacturers (OEMs) that produce cars, trucks, and SUVs, or within the supplier base, the ability of the industry to consolidate is not just about a black and white balance sheet. It is far more about the organization and having systems in place that can handle the doubling of a company's size and an expansion of products and services, yet still deliver quality products on time. These are products that will incorporate new technologies and useful features that must completely fulfill customers' needs. Where the industry stumbles the most with consolidation is probably in the human network and the operating systems (including a broad systems engineering approach) that handle different personalities of companies merging, rather than in the actual merging of the balance sheet.

Finally, closely connected to the economy is the environment. The issues moving forward are enormous: What does an automotive company do to make its products compatible with the environment? How do we deal with the global energy crisis? How do we plan new models around cities and urban life? For instance, in Europe and Asia, they have different needs because of the way those communities have grown and developed. Automakers have to work hard to find what fits well within their systems and cultures.

A great example that encompasses the environment-, economy-, culture-, and technology-driven themes I have just mentioned is the topic of bringing diesel engines to the U.S. passenger car market. Diesel technology in passenger cars has come a long way over the years, especially due to its popularity in Europe. These engines offer tremendous fuel efficiency and with new exhaust catalysts are more environmentally friendly than traditional gasoline vehicles.

This sounds like a must-have for the U.S. market, but this technology means redefining the driving experience. The issues are tremendous.

To start, the U.S. culture has a negative opinion of diesel because of poorly engineered engines in the recent past. Also, the marketplace currently lacks a clean diesel fuel infrastructure to support these engines. These are just some of the key issues that must be considered before defining a business case for automakers to bring diesel-engine passenger cars to the market. It proves exactly how complex the automotive industry is today. To me, all of these issues represent different challenges for the industry. But the key factor imbedded in all of them is that customers' expectations continue to rise.

Strategies for Success

In terms of personal success, I always tell others: If you do not have passion for what you do, then make a change, because your lack of passion and personal enthusiasm will only result in products and services that will be less than they could be. What automakers need in the industry are people who are filled with passion and love for what they do. And if you are passionate about something, you will continue to learn; you will be a lifelong learner and a teacher.

People also need to do what they think is right, make the right decisions. This is independent of the industry, but core to the passion they feel inside. Make sure you have integrity and are making what you believe is the right decision, and be willing to challenge something if you do not think it is right. When you have those traits, you have a solid foundation to move forward.

From a corporate perspective, to thrive in the marketplace, OEMs have to understand what customers want and then be daring enough to listen and go beyond that to try new things. If we ask our customers what they would like to see three years from now, and we do exactly what they tell us, we would probably satisfy some tastes, but we would miss large portions of the customer base because projections for the future are simply not accurate. Companies such as Ford have to be daring in some areas: Go to the marketplace with new products, try different things, and push the envelope.

At the same time, OEMs have to balance customer needs with features and functions that are more conservative because not all of our potential customers want to live on the edge. One way to position for the future is to look at the product lineup, reduce the time to market, and make sure the products and services we offer are broadly scoped. There is a great opportunity to try some things that are far out and edgy and that will reach different groups and types of customers, and at the same time balance that with very high-volume products. For example, a car platform may be the basis for a high-volume vehicle meeting many peoples' transportation needs, but the same platform can also include a niche product or feature that pushes the envelope. Understanding and delivering to the customer completes one part of the puzzle.

Other key strategies for success in the automotive industry include the application of technology, which I have already touched on, reusing parts across multiple applications, and really leveraging the fixed assets and resources that automakers – and the total value delivery chain – have in place. With that comes the whole global strategy for capacity management and making sure we are responsible for our actions. When our products and services are not relevant, the impact on the communities in which we operate is enormous. Global capacity management and product relevance have to be the key levers to ensuring automakers thrive in the future.

To stay on top of things, I learn and teach. By teaching you learn, and by learning you can teach. I learn through the reading of periodicals, not just automotive but total global trends, fashion, industry, and so on. For instance, Home & Garden Television (HGTV) is a great way to see in a short period of time the foods, tastes, feelings of home and the trends people are currently enjoying in the U.S. It is an interesting channel that lets you see the broader picture.

I read all of the automotive periodicals, but I tend to read things outside of the automotive publications because I think there are many things that influence potential customers. I feel industry magazines miss some people's thoughts and feelings. I also look at both international and local papers.

I am also tied to Stanford University through recruiting and The Stanford Alliance for Integrated Manufacturing that has consortiums with several major manufacturing companies that operate globally. I am on the board of directors of Automotive Alliance Industries (a joint venture with Ford and Mazda) and work with the nonprofit sector (Focus Hope, local church activities).

I believe individuals in the automotive industry really need to try to take all these global and holistic experiences and then apply them every day. The industry needs to be asking itself, Are we making the best decisions we possibly can? Are we doing the right things? Are they sustainable?

Creating effective teams is also a critical component of success. Putting together a vehicle, from concept into production, is a huge effort with large teams that are typically widely dispersed. You might have 100 people working side by side in one building down the hall from you, but then out in the supply base and their manufacturers, the number builds to thousands of individuals who are all working to bring one car or truck to the market. For example, with the recent launch of a sporty rear-wheel-drive convertible, I was in charge of 150 people directly and influencing 1,200 individuals throughout the supply base.

We have to make sure we have the right balance between incredibly competent technical people and those with a wealth of real-world experience. Individual teams need to balance enthusiasm with risk management. They also need to balance talent with management and technical challenges. Let's look at how companies like Ford do this.

When Ford management puts a team together, we look at three views of each team member. First we do a Myers-Briggs personality assessment. Second, management examines a talent survey, which looks at our inherent talents and strengths. Third, we look at learned skills and knowledge. We combine these elements and look at the strengths of our business and for blind spots in certain areas. We look to see how we can adjust within the group, to fill the voids, and if necessary, we turn to the outside to complete the team.

The really important thing about putting teams together is making sure you have a balance of views, innate talents, and learned knowledge and skills, and that you value the diversity everybody brings to the table. Then you get the best decisions and have the ability to do the impossible. When you have the right mix of people together, and your goals are clear, the project will succeed. If a team comes across two or three things where we just cannot get a breakthrough, then I know the team needs an adjustment, a catalyst to rejuvenate creativity.

Looking Toward the Future

The big drivers of change historically have been and always will be the environment and the cost of operating vehicles, which is inherently driven by fuel prices, cost of ownership, and changes in the needs of personal mobility. These issues drive enormous changes, especially with new technology. Another major item that is driving change and will continue to be a big driver in the automotive industry is safety, which I have already briefly mentioned. Finally, you have to take traffic congestion into the picture.

As populations increase with tremendous density in certain areas, the auto industry will have to help define alternatives for personal mobility and develop new solutions that will still work within over-populated communities. Once again, transportation will have to fit seamlessly into the mix.

I spend quite a bit of time in my vehicle, and much of this is simply the time to get from point A to point B. I realize that as congestion increases, solutions will have to be drafted, whether that means better lane management or new technologies that tell drivers when to turn. Ultimately, the industry will evaluate heavily congested areas, infrastructure, and the industry's entire outlook of what personal mobility is and how the automotive industry as a whole delivers it. Areas of interest to me are mobility solutions for local transit in vacation areas, shopping, and schools. I ask myself how a culture will adjust in these local travel destinations after an alternative is created. I also wonder how each individual will continue to redefine personal freedom and how I, as part of the automotive industry, can help each person fulfill their vision.

Other trends are more obvious, such as changing tastes and personalities. The public's thoughts about what a car, truck, or SUV should look like will shape the future of automotive design.

Once again I need to stress that economic pressure and consolidation on a worldwide scale and how capacity is managed will also be a dominant theme in the future. At the moment, we have an industry with excess capacity around the globe. The separation between income levels – between the haves and the have-nots – continues to grow, with fewer and fewer people falling worldwide into what we call the "middle class." This situation will change the types of products and services automakers offer, as well as the kind of jobs, training, and education that need to be provided, not only for individuals working in the automotive industry, but on a more general basis, as well. These changes and broader trends are what the industry needs to keep in mind. I cannot help wondering what a car or truck will look like in the distant future.

Environmental standards are good. What we are trying to do, as a company, is to not be driven by the standards, but to think beyond them. The resources we use up and the waste automakers create – the industry as a whole and in the community – will have to be dealt with, and most likely our children will face the majority of the burden. The good news is that we realize these issues now and as an industry need to proactively find solutions to these problems. There are always tradeoffs, though. For example, if we can reduce weight, we may alter the safety of the vehicles. We need breakthroughs to support the need for the industry to continue to push forward with lighter and lighter materials that provide improved fuel economy and performance in crash conditions.

The other part of the environment that automakers also have a tremendous amount of impact on and are paying very close attention to is not just the output of the vehicles, but our factories and supplier factories that are used in the process of making various components. So the question becomes, How can we create products throughout the whole system and add less waste to the value delivery chain? For instance, the industry needs to produce fewer byproducts from the design and assembly line process. I recall how Henry Ford specified hole locations on wooden part crates. These crates were then disassembled and became floorboards for Model Ts. Now that represents a great example of re-use and waste elimination.

So I go back to the bigger question of how we as automakers can run plants more efficiently, build more to schedule exactly what we want, and be more flexible. Then automakers can cut back on inventory and process wastes. What the industry is focused on doing is to reduce, reuse, and recycle. If waste elimination is foremost in our mindset, and every action produces something of value and minimizes waste, it is a huge lever for manufacturers and society. Clearly automakers have to work on powertrains, power plants, fuel, emissions, and safety improvements without compromising the needs of the customer. These are foremost in our minds, but the bigger lever is to think of the hundreds of factories, trucks, trains, businesses, and offices that are combined in the auto industry, and make sure the industry keeps the right mindset of waste elimination.

The whole idea of waste elimination is so fundamental to the Japanese. It simply has to be because the society lives on an island with a population half the size of the U.S. and an overall area the size of Texas. So their community and environment are driven by a totally different set of rules. In the U.S. we are blessed with quite a bit of space and quite a large number of natural resources. The open air, the freedom, and the entrepreneurial mindset we have are an outgrowth of who and what we are and our culture. It will take significant events to change behavior patterns and make consumers switch from the favored SUVs and larger cars that are not as fuel-efficient. It will take time to see us move toward a trend of using automobiles more like the smaller ones found in Europe and Asia.

In the next five or ten years, what happens in global fuel pricing will have a huge impact on the automotive industry. Congestion and how we as a society, whether in the U.S. or elsewhere in the world, choose to deal with it will have a major impact on personal mobility. The availability of materials in the future will be another area of concern. Today this is exemplified in the steel industry. The steel industry is struggling in the U.S., and we therefore now have to go global sources. The end game problem is that steel is big and heavy, so transport prices go up.

The continued divergence of the social wealth, with the haves and the have-nots, has proved to be a lasting trend. Certainly with the markets the way they are today (and depending upon how they rebound), the differences in income levels, both worldwide and in the U.S., will have a tremendous impact on what potential customers view as affordable. Environmental trends will continue, as will safety trends. The one thing I do not think will change is the emotion that cars, trucks, and SUVs evoke, and the desire of people to have vehicles they will connect with.

I imagine when I reach an age close to that of my great aunt when she died, that driving and personal mobility, freedom of mind and distances, will still be an emotional experience. It will probably be very different from what it is now, but I know that society's passion for automobiles will never die. With all these different forces acting on the industry as a whole, there is no doubt in my mind that the work I do today to find the next breakthrough in personal mobility will help define the distant future of the automotive industry.

Nancy Lee Gioia was appointed vehicle line director of Lifestyle Vehicles in December 2001. Her responsibilities include product creation leadership for the Windstar, Mustang, and Thunderbird vehicle lines, with annual revenue responsibilities of approximately $10 billion.

Ms. Gioia joined Ford Motor Company in June 1982 as a graduate trainee in the Electronics Division. From 1983 to 1986, she held various positions in the Electronic Division's Powertrain business unit. In June 1986, she became manufacturing and quality engineer at the Engine

Control Electronics manufacturing facility in Lansdale, Pennsylvania.

Before becoming the supervisor for Powertrain Electronic Controls Engineering in 1989, she was the liaison engineer in the Electronics Division Product Engineering Office for Ford's new Cadiz, Spain, manufacturing facility.
In June 1991, Ms. Gioia was named alliance manager for the Electronics Division, responsible for the management, development, and growth of strategic alliances. In February 1993, she became a manufacturing and materials manager, promoted later that year to manager of Assembly Operations in the Climate Control Division at Ford's Plymouth, Michigan, plant.

In August 1994, Ms. Gioia was named chief engineer – Commercial Truck, Automotive Components Division and in February 1996 was appointed chief program engineer for the Louisville/AeroMax truck line.

Before her current appointment, she served as chief program engineer for the all-new Ford Thunderbird.

In July 2001 Ms. Gioia received the All Star Award from Automotive News.

Ms. Gioia received her bachelor's degree in electrical engineering from the University of Michigan and her Master of Sciences in Manufacturing Systems Engineering (MSMSE) from Stanford University. While studying with the assistance of a Ford Advanced Education Fellowship, she received the Outstanding Service Award from the Stanford Institute for Manufacturing and Automation.

MEETING THE DEMANDS OF TOMORROW'S CONSUMERS

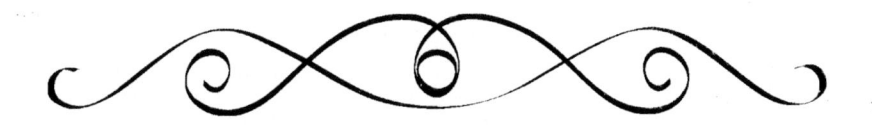

RICHARD COLLIVER

American Honda Motor Co., Inc.

Executive Vice President, Automobile Sales

Automotive Trends and Changes

The American consumer is in love with the automobile and is fascinated by the manufacturing side. It is easy to go to any kind of public function and start talking to someone who wants to talk about cars. They want to be your friend once they find you are involved with the automobile industry.

The automotive business is very, very exciting. There are rapid changes every day, in terms of consumer perceptions or desires, the product, and the market. When I look back at the product and the way it has evolved over the years, from the time I entered the business in the early 1960s to where we are today, I see it has changed tremendously – not only in terms of styling and safety, but also in terms of efficiency and quality. The industry has become more environmentally conscious and is developing products that are more versatile and dependable.

Today, automakers must be more sensitive to environmental issues, whether they are clean air or consumption of fuel. Consumer environmental concerns, from gas mileage to the type of fuel used, will continue to become more important. These issues will continue to change the industry and the size of the product we will drive in the future. We will see a larger segment of our automobile market buying smaller vehicles. Hybrid technologies will also become more mainstream. We have hybrid fuel-cell technology we will test on the streets of U.S. cities next year; this technology will be mainstream within five years.

Over the last few decades, the biggest product change has been improvement based on consumer demands. We listen to the consumer. Manufacturers have responded to the consumer with a product of higher quality and greater dependability. Dependability, reliability, and quality (DRQ) are the keys to success. Today's consumers are more demanding.

In terms of vehicle popularity, most forecasters believe SUVs will be around for a while. They replaced station wagons a few years ago. Most of the forecast data I see show the SUV market continuing to be strong. We see migration between sedans and SUVs, and we see the SUV buyer going back to sedans. I don't believe the SUV market will continue to grow, as the segments will start to soften some on the top end. People buy an SUV because it is fun to drive; however, the versatility is not as great as some people think it is, and there's a tradeoff between initial cost and operating cost. People will again start shifting from a "me" car to a "we" car.

Years ago we had an old saying that the difference between a two-wheel- and a four-wheel-drive car is 100 yards in the mud. Ninety percent of the people who drive SUVs never take them off-road. They drive them primarily on normal streets and highways, the same way you drive a passenger car. The way you market SUVs is different today than a few years ago. In the past, SUVs had to be bouncing along dirt roads with rocks and mud flying everywhere. Today we don't see them being driven in that kind of environment. You see them driving in the country or in snow, but it is just driving in the snow, not in any wild environment. They are demonstrating SUVs in extreme weather conditions to project safety and comfort. Many SUV buyers are looking for vehicles that have the comfort, convenience, and ride of a passenger car.

Industry Challenges

Manufacturers must find ways to drive costs down and be more efficient with the products. Some of this can be accomplished through greater efficiency in the use of their manufacturing facilities. The consumer will not continue to pay higher prices. It is the role of manufactures to find ways to drive costs down. Honda has been able to change the manufacturing processes to not only speed up the efficiency but also give us the ability to build multiple types of cars on the same production line without a major investment. Flexibility and speed are key. We have been able to cut the time, or man-hours, it takes to build a vehicle, which reduces the cost. Automation in the manufacturing process will have to increase to streamline these processes.

Another challenge that automakers face is the consumer reaction you might receive from any marketing campaign undertaken. Consumers are very quick to tell you if you missed a mark with your marketing efforts. You must target your strengths and stay focused.

Dealer retail sales is one of the most difficult areas in the retail auto industry. We must try to change the culture of the dealership showroom, so that the salespeople listen to customer needs and respond to issues instead of attempting to confuse the customer into not really knowing what they are purchasing. You must deal with customers in a very honest and open way today, but trying to get people to change their old habits is very difficult. You find some spillover even when you're dealing with Internet sales. The salespeople try to confuse customers or force them to buy. Changing the dealership management culture is a huge issue. I would like to say to all salespeople and dealers that if they went into a Nordstrom or Bloomingdale's and were treated the way they treat people, they wouldn't consider buying from those retail stores.

Consumers determine what they want to purchase using the Internet or other sources to research the types of products available. Usually consumers have identified what brand and model of car they want to purchase, and dealers need to stay focused on that. Eighty percent of our buyers use the Internet to gather information before they go into a dealership. They're a lot better prepared than they used to be. We find that if our salespeople aren't prepared to deal with these customers, and they don't contact them quickly, these Internet shoppers will buy where they get the quickest service.

A Multinational Company with a Common Culture

Although we're part of a multinational company, American Honda operates as a separate entity from Honda Motor Company. American Honda has our own marketing, sales, and product planning for the Americas. While we work globally within the company, we don't work globally externally. We source automobiles from 11 or 12 plants – some in Europe, some in Asia, and some in North America, from Canada to Mexico. We manage based on the philosophy that we develop and market our products in the markets where we're located. We stay focused on just the North American market.

We have a dedicated sales and production planning group that manages all the various plants on scheduling. We have Japanese coordinators to assist, should we have a communication problem. It's a full-time job. One group may work with the plants in Ohio; one may work with the plants in Canada; and another with the plants in Asia. Honda has standardized all our systems worldwide – our various e-mail and communication devices all around the world – so we all talk in the same language in the same format for effective and speedy communication..

Honda has been very successful in establishing a common culture across the world in all our facilities. The Honda philosophy was written by our founder, Soichiro Honda, in 1948. It's the way we do business, how we relate to the associates who work for us, and how we relate to the people outside our company. It really is a pretty easy common denominator. You can go from one country to another and find the same operating philosophies and managing styles.

Management and Leadership

My management style is very open and approachable. People understand what I expect, and I let my managers manage the core parts of their business. I use MBWA – Management By Walking Around. Communication is extremely important. I expect my direct reports to keep me advised of their processes and the work they are doing. I believe in work in progress.

I see three things that are critical for managers: You must listen when people talk. You need a strong ability to communicate to your associates. And they have to continue to gather research information so they are up to speed on past, current, and future trends. Also, managers must be smart, but the ability to communicate and listen to people is particularly critical.

Demonstrating leadership to the work force within the company is very important. A leader with charisma is someone you can go to – someone you have confidence in and believe in, and who has the ability to communicate and make things happen.

To be a long-term successful leader, you must be honest. You must believe in your company and what your tasks are. You must believe your business strategies are right, but never be afraid to say "No" or "Stop." Always be flexible and be prepared to change.

As Forrest Gump says, "Life's like a box of chocolates. You never know what you're gonna get."

Richard E. Colliver is executive vice president of American Honda Motor Co., Inc., heading both Honda and Acura Automobile Divisions, and is a member of the American Honda Board of Directors. Mr. Colliver is responsible for U.S. sales activities of the Honda and Acura Divisions, as well as Acura Parts and Service field operations. In addition, he oversees Honda and Acura market representation, customer marketing, dealer business management, and product and sales information.

Mr. Colliver joined Honda in 1993 as senior vice president of the Honda Automobile Division. In 1997, he was promoted to executive vice president and appointed to the board of directors. In 1998 he assumed responsibilities for the Acura Division.

Under Mr. Colliver's leadership, the Honda Division has set sales records in each of the last three years, and Honda dealers are among the most profitable in the industry.

Before joining Honda, Mr. Colliver enjoyed a career of more than 20 years with Mazda Motors of America, where he rose through the ranks from district manager to group vice president and general manager. During his tenure at Mazda, he held various executive positions in vehicle and parts distribution, business planning, dealer placement, dealer operations, and feasibility analysis for new product lines. Before joining Mazda, Mr. Colliver's automotive career, which began in 1962, included a number of sales and marketing positions with General Motors and Chrysler.

Born and raised in Coffeyville, Kansas, Mr. Colliver graduated in 1962 from Pittsburg State University in Kansas with a Bachelor of Science degree in business administration. He completed the Wharton School Advanced Management Program at the University of Pennsylvania in 1992.

THE BIG PICTURE: UNDERSTANDING CUSTOMER EXPECTATIONS

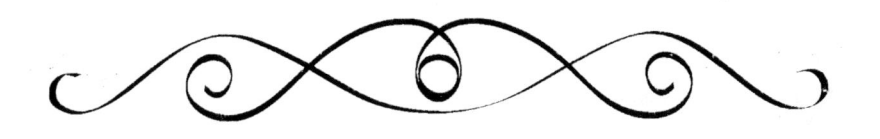

J. D. POWER, III

J. D. Power and Associates

Chairman and Chief Executive Officer

The Effects of Competition

The ever-increasing availability of information, largely due to the Internet, enables consumers to be more informed than ever before. Today consumers have higher expectations and are more knowledgeable when it comes to negotiating at the dealership. As the automotive marketplace becomes even more competitive and quality and customer satisfaction continue to improve, the abundance of consumer choices means the industry will face significant changes ahead. From vehicle design to distribution, the voice of the customer is becoming increasingly important in shaping the automotive industry. This has not always been the case.

During the late 1960s and early 1970s, the industry went through a particularly difficult time. As a result of poor vehicle quality and poor service at the dealership, Congress enacted a wave of government regulations to protect the consumer interest. Based on these regulations, numerous recalls were instituted to address poor vehicle quality. In this manufacturing-driven environment, engineers determined which models would be produced and what features would be offered. Consumer perceptions of quality and satisfaction, as well as their intentions and expectations, were not considered. Many automotive executives in Detroit believed consumers were not sophisticated enough to make judgments regarding vehicle quality, and this critical error left the industry vulnerable to foreign competition.

Increased competition for Detroit soon arrived in the form of smaller, less expensive, and more fuel-efficient vehicles from Japan. At first Detroit simply dismissed the foreign manufacturers as unworthy competitors, believing American consumers would not be attracted to Japanese-made vehicles. However, they were soon proved wrong as the foreign competitors increased in popularity, especially because of the energy crisis in the early 1970s.

Over time, the Big Three manufacturers (Chrysler, Ford, and General Motors) began to realize they had to increase quality and customer satisfaction to stay in business. And to some extent, they are still coming to grips with the effects of foreign competition. A more recent example of this phenomenon is the impact Lexus has had during its relatively short history. As a newcomer in 1989, many in the industry believed Lexus posed little threat. In the intervening years, Lexus redefined the customer satisfaction experience and became recognized for producing vehicles with industry-leading quality levels. Consequently, the bar was raised for all manufacturers. To illustrate this, the quality levels of the industry leader in 1982 – Mercedes-Benz – would today be considered only average.

A Revolution in Automotive Distribution

With regard to cutting costs on the retail side of the business, the automotive industry has not evolved significantly in the past three decades. Industry statistics indicate there is approximately $100-$120 billion of inefficiency within the automotive distribution system. Distribution costs, which account for nearly one-third of the cost of the average car or truck in the U.S., include sales and marketing, contests and incentives, inventory, warranty, and transportation and dealer costs, among others. Also included is approximately $40 billion annually for incentives and rebates; $15 billion for advertising these incentives and driving traffic to retailer locations; and an additional $50 billion in finished-goods inventory. Manufacturers spend billions of dollars annually in the United States providing incentives to encourage the purchase of new vehicles.

To counteract this expense, manufacturers could benefit greatly from using point-of-sale transaction data, which would allow them to use incentives more effectively, understand purchasing behavior more clearly, and compare dealer performance nationwide. Companies in the consumer packaged goods, pharmaceutical, and recording industries use point-of-sale transaction data to increase sales and profits and reduce costs. POS data allows them to develop more effective pricing strategies, create more efficient advertising and promotional campaigns, increase manufacturing efficiency, lower inventory costs through improved supply chain management, and reduce distribution costs through automated reordering based on consumer-driven demand.

An example of this point-of-sale concept is the Universal Product Code System (UPC) and retail scanning system that was adopted 30 years ago by such powerhouses as General Foods, General Mills, and Kraft and that controlled the packaged goods industry. Since there was no organized system for managing inventory, products often languished in the storeroom, while grocery store shelves remained empty. This system was wasteful and inefficient, but it was the best available at the time. With the advent of the UPC system, which provided a bar code on each product, the packaged goods industry took a major step forward, and retailers were able to track the movement of products through the distribution system. At the retail level, however, the key technology was the scanning system that recorded each product transaction on a real-time basis.

The widespread use of scanning data allowed retailers to accurately determine revenue and profitability. It revolutionized the packaged goods industry by providing profitability measures and helped retailers determine the right mix of products. Almost overnight, retailers gained a powerful tool to increase efficiency and cut costs. Consumers benefited through lower prices and product selection that more closely matched demand.

Applying this technology in the automotive industry would give retailers more power to dictate to the manufacturers what products are needed and at what price points. We believe this capability is just on the horizon. J.D. Power and Associates has taken the point-of-sale transaction data concept and adapted it to the automotive industry with its Power Information Network (PIN). Through PIN, we compile dealer transaction data on a daily basis and provide aggregated results to subscribing dealers in real time. The benefits PIN brings to the automotive industry are similar to the efficiency improvements the packaged goods industry realized by adopting the UPC system 30 years ago.

Trends in the Automotive Industry

The abundance of information available today levels the playing field between consumers and dealers. Consumers now have access to the same information dealers used to keep to themselves. We're seeing a trend toward the elimination of the negotiating process because more and more people are getting reliable, timely information. We're not yet at the point where price negotiation is a thing of the past, but certain retailers, such as Saturn, do so well in sales satisfaction because they have eliminated this contentious issue from the car-buying process. Overall, I think the automotive industry has been quite resistant to that concept, but there has certainly been a reduction in the variance of what people pay for a vehicle. Because the invoice price and MSRP are now readily available, consumers are much more aware of the acceptable price range for any particular vehicle and less likely to be taken advantage of by the salesperson.

Our research indicates the average Internet user is more informed when purchasing a vehicle than ever before.

Many times, they go into the dealerships knowing more than the salesperson who meets them at the door. This changes the balance of power. The consumer isn't sold a vehicle that the salesperson wants to sell; the consumer buys what he wants. Increasingly, consumers know what they want when they walk in, and if the dealer doesn't have it, they'll go elsewhere.

A popular segment of the automotive industry that really surprised me is the rapid acceptance of SUVs, a segment of the market that is still expanding. Virtually every manufacturer is participating in this segment, and it will become even more competitive over the next few years. I think we'll see a steady market out there, but with everyone participating in it, the profits manufacturers have enjoyed over the past five or six years will be reduced because of increased competition.

Concern about environmental issues is another key trend. I believe the automotive industry has been doing a very good job with regard to environmental issues. In our current situation, where many people want big cars and big SUVs, it's remarkable that the fuel economy has improved as much as it has.

I think the industry is trying very hard to meet the needs of the consumer. Where we have the problem, I believe, is in terms of the democratic process in the U.S., with the legislators calling the shots. No one wants to increase the tax on gasoline because that would hurt the working person, the transportation of goods, and the pricing of vehicles.

I believe you can't come up with regulations to create more fuel-efficient, smaller vehicles. There needs to be a system where the marketplace directs the consumer – through the pricing mechanism – to conserve fuel. Then you would have more people interested in hybrid vehicles (with improved gas mileage) because they could see it is more economical to purchase that type of vehicle. That is where the legislature has to effectively enact laws, rules, and regulations that will force the market-pricing mechanism to take over and change consumer behavior, rather than the government telling the manufacturers to build vehicles that have better fuel economy.

One of the biggest ironies I see is that as the industry continues to improve the dependability and durability of its vehicles, the net effect is that we're adding to the vehicle population at a significant rate. We have too many cars on the road, and the biggest shortcoming is the infrastructure – there are not enough freeways and traffic systems. Travel times are increasing at an alarming rate, and people are spending more time in their vehicles, which does not help fuel economy or the economy in general, because of lower productivity. I think the government has to put effort into the infrastructure on a national, state, and local basis to improve the efficiency of our automotive transportation system.

Automotive Industry Leaders

Leaders are people who can think "outside the box" and work on being innovative within the realities of the marketplace, rather than trying to stick to systems that were more appropriate 40 or 50 years ago. People who understand the big picture, think strategically, and listen to what the customer is saying will stand out and be more successful. Customer satisfaction is based on understanding consumer expectations and meeting them. Although the automotive industry has made great strides in the last 20 years in vehicle quality and customer satisfaction, I think we will see more of that in the coming years.

I advise leaders to keep ahead of the wave, but be careful not to get crushed by it. And, if you get too far out in front, you might get swept away by the current.

It's also important to open up your thinking. Look at the world around you and see what others are doing. Other industries move faster because they don't have the tradition of the automotive industry, which is much more manufacturing-oriented. I advise people to look at the big picture and realize that the automotive industry isn't that much different from other industries. The competitive nature of the business demands a broader perspective, which is a key ingredient to their future success.

J. D. Power, III, has spent more than 40 years as a pioneer in customer satisfaction work, with the last 34 as founder of what has become one of the most prestigious marketing information firms in the world – J. D. Power and Associates. The firm numbers among its clients virtually every automotive manufacturer and importer serving the U.S. market, in addition to clients in many other industries and around the world. With corporate headquarters in Westlake Village, California, the firm has regional offices in Orange, California; Detroit, Michigan; Phoenix, Arizona; and Westport, Connecticut, and international offices in Toronto, Tokyo, London, Singapore, and Sydney.

Mr. Power was appointed chairman and chief executive officer of J. D. Power and Associates in August 1996. He frequently speaks to top management and boards of directors of companies worldwide. The firm's reputation as a premier resource of customer satisfaction data and consultancies has led to research and projects in a variety of industries, including automotive, financial services, telecommunications (cable, cellular, and local and long-distance telephone), travel, home builder, utilities, and healthcare.

Following graduation from College of the Holy Cross in 1953, Mr. Power served four years of line officer duty aboard a Coast Guard icebreaker in the Arctic and the Antarctic. He subsequently earned an MBA from the Wharton School of Finance at the University of Pennsylvania. He joined Ford Motor Company as a financial analyst and later worked for Marplan as a marketing research consultant for General Motors Corporation's Buick and GMC truck and coach divisions. Before launching J. D. Power and Associates in 1968, Mr. Power worked as a marketing research executive for J. I. Case Company, a construction and farm equipment manufacturer, and was director of corporate planning for McCulloch Corporation, a Los Angeles-based engine manufacturer.

In 1992 Mr. Power received the Automotive Hall of Fame's Distinguished Service Citation, awarded each year to seven of the industry's most accomplished leaders. He holds *honorary doctorate degrees from College of the Holy Cross; California Lutheran University; California State University, Northridge; and College Misericordia. He also serves as an adjunct professor of marketing at California State University, Northridge.*

Spend 5 minutes on the phone with one of our Business Editors...

and we can guarantee we will identify a way to give you or your company an edge, or find a more time efficient way to help you stay ahead of the curve on any business topic. For more information and ideas on how we can help you stay ahead of the curve, please call an Aspatore Business Editor at 1-866-Aspatore.

Call 1-8<u>66</u>-Aspatore

To Order or For Customized Suggestions From an Aspatore Business Editor, Please Call 1-8<u>66</u>-Aspatore (277-2867) Or Visit www.Aspatore.com

BUSINESS INTELLIGENCE PUBLICATIONS & SERVICES

THE C-LEVEL LIBRARY

Empower yourself and your company with an expansive web-based library featuring hundreds of books, briefs and articles - all available in multiple formats - written by C-Level executives, and published by Aspatore. Available exclusively from Aspatore, The C-Level Library is the largest of its kind, and featuring the most extensive collection of C-Level content in the world, it is the ultimate reference tool. Such a resource enables you and your team to speak intelligently with anyone from any industry, on any topic. Every year, Aspatore publishes C-Level executives from over half the Global 500, the fastest-growing 250 private companies, MP/Chairs from over half the 250 largest law firms and consulting firms, and leading executives representing nearly every industry. Content is updated weekly and available for use in various formats - as-is online, printed, copied and pasted into a PDA, and even emailed directly to you. The C-Level Library enables you and your team to quickly get up to speed on a topic, understand key issues driving an industry, identify new ideas for business opportunities, and profit from the knowledge of the world's leading executives. To see a sample main navigation page, please visit www.aspatore.com/elibray4.asp.

Titles in One Industry Only
i) Electronic access to publications in one specialty area (Select from: Technology, Legal, Entrepreneurial/Venture Capital, Marketing/Advertising/PR, Management/Consulting, Health, Reference) (Via Password Protected Web Site)
Individual Pricing - $99 a month (1 Year Minimum)
Corporate Pricing - $499 a month (1 Year Minimum), $399 a month (2 Years Minimum), $249 a month (5 Year Minimum), Price includes up to 20 user seats (individuals that can access the site, both employees and customers), Each additional seat is $25 a month

Access to All Titles
ii) Electronic access to receive every publication published by Aspatore a year. Approximately 60-70 books a year and hundreds of other publications
Individual Pricing - $149 a month (1 Year Minimum)
Corporate Pricing - $999 a month (1 Year Minimum), $899 a month (2 Years Minimum), $699 a month (5 Year Minimum), Price includes up to 20 user seats (individuals that can access the site, both employees and customers), Each additional seat is $35 a month

Access to All Titles With Additional Navigation
iii) Same as ii, however all publications are arranged by different divisions of your company, each with its own web site. Upon order, you will receive an email from our editors about setting up a time to discuss navigation for your business.
Corporate Pricing - $1999 a month (1 Year Minimum), $1799 a month (2 Years Minimum), $1399 a month (5 Year Minimum), Price includes up to 20 overall user seats and up to 10 different web sites, Each additional seat is $45 a month

To Order or For Customized Suggestions From an Aspatore Business Editor, Please Call 1-866-Aspatore (277-2867) Or Visit www.Aspatore.com

THE FOCUSBOOK ™ — YOUR CUSTOMIZED BOOK IN PRINT

Receive a custom book based on your Business Intelligence Profile, with content from all new books, essays and other publications by Aspatore from the quarter that fits your area of specialty. The content is from over 100 publications (books, essays, journals, briefs) on various industries, positions, and topics, available to you months before the general public. Each custom book ranges between 180-280. Up to 50 pages of text can be added in each book, enabling you to further customize the book for particular practice groups, teams, new hires or even clients. Put your company name on the front cover and give your books a title, if you like.

For Individuals $129 One Time, $99 a Quarter (1 Year Minimum) (Includes 1 Book a Quarter) For Corporations and Multiple Books, Please call 1-866-Aspatore (277-2867) or Visit www.Aspatore.com for pricing

EXECENABLERS ™ — GET UP TO SPEED FAST!

ExecEnablers help you determine what to read so that you can get up to speed on a new topic fast, with the right books, magazines, web sites, and other publications (from over 30,000 business publishing sources). The 2-step process involves an approximately 30 minute phone call and then a report written by Aspatore Business Editors and mailed (or emailed) to you the following day (rush/same day options available-please call 1-866-Aspatore). Only $49 Perfect for new hires....

ASPATORE C-LEVEL RESEARCH ™

Aspatore Business Editors are available to help individuals, companies, and professionals in any industry perform research on a given topic on either a one-time or a consistent monthly basis. Aspatore Business Editors, with their deep industry expertise at getting access to the right information across every medium, can serve as an external librarian/researcher for all your research needs. For more information, please email store@aspatore.com or call us at 1-866-Aspatore.

ESTABLISH YOUR OWN BUSINESS/REFERENCE LIBRARY ™

Work with Aspatore editors to identify 50-5,000 individual books from all publishers, and purchase them at special rates for a corporate or personal library. Employ Aspatore as an external librarian for all your research needs. For more information, please email store@aspatore.com or call us at 1-866-Aspatore.

PIA (PERSONAL INTELLIGENCE AGENT) ™ — CUSTOM READING LISTS

PIA Reports provide you, your company, or a division/group within it, with information on exactly where to find additional business intelligence from newly published books, articles, speeches, journals, magazines, web sites and over 30,000 other business intelligence sources (from every major business publisher in the world) that match your

To Order or For Customized Suggestions From an Aspatore Business Editor, Please Call 1-866-Aspatore (277-2867) Or Visit www.Aspatore.com

areas of interest. Each 8-10 page report features sections on the most important new books, articles, and speeches to read, descriptions of each, approximate reading times/page counts, and information on the author and publication sources, so you can decide what you should read and how to spend your time most efficiently. Please call 1-866-Aspatore to speak with an Aspatore Business Editor to identify your areas of interest so the PIA Report can be customized specifically to your areas of interest.

For Individuals, $99 a Year for 4 Quarterly Reports, Copies Not Permitted
For 1 Report For Entire Company, $499 a Year for 4 Quarterly Reports, Copies Permitted
(Reports arrive within two weeks of start of each quarter.)
For Multiple Reports For Same Company, Please call 1-866-Aspatore (277-2867)

THE C-LEVEL REVIEW ™

The C-Level Review is an essay based review that helps you maximize your strengths as a professional through the personal recommendations of leading C-Level executives (CEOs, CFOs, CTOs, CMOs, Partners, Lawyers (Chairs and MPs). Perfect for professionals of all levels and in all industries, the review takes one to three hours to complete, and you remain anonymous to the panel members, each of whom reviews your answers and provides a critical analysis of areas where you should focus your career efforts. Your results are compiled in a 10-20 page report, with separate reviews written by three C-level executives. The C-Level Review Panel, a highly prestigious group of authors published by Aspatore, includes C-Level executives from some of the world's largest and most respected companies. As they review your essay answers, they will identify ways to help you enhance your strengths, eliminate your weaknesses, and pinpoint where to focus your talents. Anonymous to both sides, the C-Level Review is an exceptional opportunity for professionals of all levels to get personalized, insider career guidance and recommendations from the world's most respected executives.

Only $499-Books are mailed within 3 days of purchase and can be completed in print-right in the book- or electronic format-in email or in Microsoft Word. Once the test is completed and mailed back to Aspatore, please allow 4-6 weeks for review to be mailed back.) Separate tests are available for management, consulting, technology, law, marketing, advertising, public relations, and entrepreneurship.

LICENSE CONTENT PUBLISHED BY ASPATORE

For information on licensing content published by Aspatore for a web site, corporate intranet, extranet, newsletter, direct mail, book or in another format, please email store@aspatore.com.

BULK ORDERS OF BOOKS & CHAPTER EXCERPTS

For information on bulk purchases of books or chapter excerpts (specific chapters within a book, bound as their own mini-book) or to develop your own book based on any content published by Aspatore, please email store@aspatore.com. For orders over 100 books or chapter excerpts, company logos and additional text can be added to the book. Use for sales and marketing, direct mail and trade show work.

To Order or For Customized Suggestions From an Aspatore Business Editor, Please Call 1-866-Aspatore (277-2867) Or Visit www.Aspatore.com

Best Selling Books
(Also Available Individually At Your Local Bookstore)

REFERENCE

Business Travel Bible (BTB) – Must Have Information for Business Travelers
Business Grammar, Style & Usage – Rules for Articulate and Polished Business Writing and Speaking
ExecRecs – Executive Recommendations For The Best Products, Services & Intelligence Executives Use to Excel
The C-Level Test – Business IQ & Personality Test for Professionals of All Levels
The Business Translator-Business Words, Phrases & Customs in Over 90 Languages

MANAGEMENT/CONSULTING

Leading CEOs – CEOs Reveal the Secrets to Leadership & Profiting in Any Economy
Leading Consultants – Industry Leaders Share Their Knowledge on the Art of Consulting
Recession Profiteers – How to Profit in a Recession & Wipe Out the Competition
Managing & Profiting in a Down Economy – Leading CEOs Reveal the Secrets to Increased Profits and Success in a Turbulent Economy
Leading Women – What It Takes to Succeed & Have It All in the 21st Century
Become a CEO – The Golden Rules to Rising the Ranks of Leadership
Leading Deal Makers – Leveraging Your Position and the Art of Deal Making
The Art of Deal Making – The Secrets to the Deal Making Process
Empower Profits – The Secrets to Cutting Costs & Making Money in ANY Economy
Building an Empire – The 10 Most Important Concepts to Focus a Business on the Way to Dominating the Business World
Management Consulting Brainstormers – Question Blocks & Idea Worksheets

TECHNOLOGY

Leading CTOs – The Secrets to the Art, Science & Future of Technology
Software Product Management – Managing Software Development from Idea to Development to Marketing to Sales
The Telecommunications Industry – Leading CEOs Share Their Knowledge on The Future of the Telecommunications Industry
Know What the CTO Knows – The Tricks of the Trade and Ways for Anyone to Understand the Language of the Techies
Web 2.0 AC (After Crash) – The Resurgence of the Internet and Technology Economy
The Semiconductor Industry – Leading CEOs Share Their Knowledge on the Future of Semiconductors
Techie Talk – The Tricks of the Trade and Ways to Develop, Implement and Capitalize on the Best Technologies in the World
Technology Brainstormers – Question Blocks & Idea Development Worksheets

VENTURE CAPITAL/ENTREPRENEURIAL

Term Sheets & Valuations – A Detailed Look at the Intricacies of Term Sheets & Valuations
Deal Terms – The Finer Points of Deal Structures, Valuations, Term Sheets, Stock Options and Getting Deals Done
Leading Deal Makers – Leveraging Your Position and the Art of Deal Making
The Art of Deal Making – The Secrets to the Deal Making Process
Hunting Venture Capital – Understanding the VC Process and Capturing an Investment
The Golden Rules of Venture Capitalists – Valuing Companies, Identifying Opportunities, Detecting Trends, Term Sheets and Valuations

To Order or For Customized Suggestions From an Aspatore Business Editor, Please Call 1-866-Aspatore (277-2867) Or Visit www.Aspatore.com

Entrepreneurial Momentum – Gaining Traction for Businesses of All Sizes to Take the Step to the Next Level

The Entrepreneurial Problem Solver – Entrepreneurial Strategies for Identifying Opportunities in the Marketplace

Entrepreneurial Brainstormers – Question Blocks & Idea Development Worksheets

LEGAL

Privacy Matters – Leading Privacy Visionaries Share Their Knowledge on How Privacy on the Internet Will Affect Everyone

Leading Lawyers – Leading Managing Partners Reveal the Secrets to Professional and Personal Success as a Lawyer

The Innovative Lawyer – Leading Lawyers Share Their Knowledge on Using Innovation to Gain an Edge

Leading Labor Lawyers – Labor Chairs Reveal the Secrets to the Art & Science of Labor Law

Leading Litigators – Litigation Chairs Revel the Secrets to the Art & Science of Litigation

Leading IP Lawyers – IP Chairs Reveal the Secrets to the Art & Science of IP Law

Leading Patent Lawyers – The & Science of Patent Law

Leading Deal Makers – Leveraging Your Position and the Art of Deal Making

Legal Brainstormers – Question Blocks & Idea Development Worksheets

FINANCIAL

Textbook Finance – The Fundamentals We Should All Know (And Remember) About Finance

Know What the CFO Knows – Leading CFOs Reveal What the Rest of Us Should Know About the Financial Side of Companies

Leading Accountants – The Golden Rules of Accounting & the Future of the Accounting Industry and Profession

Leading Investment Bankers – Leading I-Bankers Reveal the Secrets to the Art & Science of Investment Banking

The Financial Services Industry – The Future of the Financial Services Industry & Professions

Empower Profits – The Secrets to Cutting Costs & Making Money in ANY Economy

MARKETING/ADVERTISING/PR

Leading Marketers – Leading Chief Marketing Officers Reveal the Secrets to Building a Billion Dollar Brand

Emphatic Marketing – Getting the World to Notice and Use Your Company

Leading Advertisers – Advertising CEOs Reveal the Tricks of the Advertising Profession

The Art of PR – Leading PR CEOs Reveal the Secrets to the Public Relations Profession

The Golden Rules of Marketing – Leading Marketers Reveal the Secrets to Marketing, Advertising and Building Successful Brands

PR Visionaries – PR CEOS Reveal the Golden Rules of PR

Textbook Marketing – The Fundamentals We Should All Know (And Remember) About Marketing

Know What the VP of Marketing Knows – What Everyone Should Know About Marketing, For the Rest of Us Not in Marketing

Marketing Brainstormers – Question Blocks & Idea Development Worksheets

Guerrilla Marketing – The Best of Guerrilla Marketing-Big Marketing Ideas For a Small Budget

The Art of Sales – The Secrets for Anyone to Become a Rainmaker and Why Everyone in a Company Should be a Salesperson

---

To Order or For Customized Suggestions From an Aspatore Business Editor, Please Call 1-866-Aspatore (277-2867) Or Visit www.Aspatore.com